GROLIER

STUDENT ENCYCLOPEDIA

VOLUME 3

BASKETBALL

CARROLL, LEWIS

GROLIER

First published 2004 by Grolier,
an imprint of Scholastic Library Publishing,
Old Sherman Turnpike
Danbury, Connecticut 06816

© 2004 Scholastic Library Publishing

Set ISBN 0-7172-5865-3
Volume ISBN 0-7172-5868-8

Library of Congress Cataloging-in-Publication Data
Grolier student encyclopedia.
          p. cm.
Includes indexes.
Summary: An encyclopedia of brief articles intended for use
by elementary school students.
   ISBN 0-7172-5865-3 (set: alk. paper)
   1. Children's encyclopedias and dictionaries. [1. Encyclopedias
and dictionaries.] I. Grolier Incorporated.
    AG5.G87 2003
    031—dc21   2003042402

For information address the publisher:
Grolier, Scholastic Library Publishing,
Old Sherman Turnpike, Danbury, Connecticut 06816

Printed and bound in Thailand

**Designed and produced by The Brown Reference Group plc
for Scholastic Library Publishing**

Project Editor:	Sally MacEachern
Designers:	Stefan Morris, Colin Tilleyloughrey
Cover Designer:	Iain Stuart
Picture Researcher:	Sharon Southren
Editors:	Clive Carpenter, Tim Footman,
	Shona Grimbly, Henry Russell,
	Gillian Sutton, Matt Turner
Maps:	Mark Walker
Illustration:	Darren Awuah
Index:	Kay Ollerenshaw
Production Director:	Alastair Gourlay
Managing Editor:	Tim Cooke
Editorial Director:	Lindsey Lowe

ABOUT THIS BOOK

The entries in this all-new 17-volume general encyclopedia are arranged alphabetically, letter by letter. So you'll find information on Alabama in Volume 1 and on Washington in Volume 17. Similarly, U.S. presidents, Canadian provinces, and countries of the world all get their own entries.

For instance, the entries on **Presidents, U.S.** (Volume 13, page 46) and the **United States of America** (Volume 16, page 43) list every president and every state, showing where you can find the specific articles about every individual president and state.

The article on **Countries of the World** (Volume 5, pages 13–14) lists every independent state in the world and gives its capital. The countries are grouped into continents, and cross-references direct you to continent entries and to those for individual countries. Population figures for the United States and Canada are based on the 2000 U.S. Census and the 2001 Canadian Census. Population figures for countries and cities outside the United States are based on mid-2000 estimates provided by the United Nations.

A special group of articles will help you with your school projects. They include book reports, debating, grammar, note taking, punctuation, research, and revision. In each case the entry gets you started and provides some helpful tips.

Each entry ends with a list of "**see also**" cross-references to other subjects in the set. They will enable you to find articles on closely related topics so you can read everything you are interested in—for instance, the slavery entry points to Abolition Movement; African Americans; Ancient Civilizations; Civil War; Confederacy; Douglass, Frederick; Emancipation Proclamation; Lincoln, Abraham; Tubman, Harriet; and United Nations.

There are two other cross-referencing devices that will also help you find information. The first are "**see**" references. They direct you from a term not used as an entry to the entry where the information will be found—for example, Rhinoceros *see* Mammal, Hoofed. The second are "**look in the index for**" references. They tell you that the set contains information about the topic and that you can find it by looking up the subject in the index. The index in every book covers all 17 volumes, so it will help you trace topics throughout the set.

Entries are illustrated with photographs, diagrams, timelines, and maps. The maps show the key geographical features, capitals, and major cities for continents, countries, states, and Canadian provinces.

Special boxes cover particular subjects in extra detail. **Key Facts** boxes give facts and figures about U.S. states, U.S. presidents, Canadian provinces, countries, and planets. **Did you know?** boxes provide detailed information about a wide range of topics. **Amazing Facts** boxes highlight fascinating or fun facts about the natural world and modern technology. **Biography** boxes introduce some of the most important architects, artists, inventors, musicians, scientists, and writers in human history.

BASKETBALL

Basketball is one of the most popular indoor sports in the world. The game was invented in 1891 by Dr. James T. Naismith. Today it is played and watched in more than 150 countries.

Basketball is a fast, exciting game that demands skilled ball play and good teamwork. It originated when Dr. Naismith, a physical education teacher in Springfield, Massachusetts, needed to keep his students occupied during the winter months. He attached a basket to the balcony at each end of the gym and established some basic rules. Since then the rules have developed, and official

A women's basketball game in Australia between the Adelaide Lightning and Perth Wildcats.

dimensions have been laid down, although court sizes may vary according to the age of the players and the size of the gym in which the game is played. Basketball can also be played on outdoor courts.

The object of the game is to get the ball into the appropriate basket (a hoop at each end of the court). Each team defends the basket at its own end of the court (the backcourt) and tries to shoot the ball into the basket at the other end (the frontcourt). The team in possession of the ball, and trying to score, is said to be on offense. The team without the ball, and trying to prevent the other team from scoring, is said to be on defense. Players can advance the ball up and down the court only by passing (throwing) it or dribbling (bouncing) it.

Players and play

There are five players on each team: a center, two forwards, and two guards. Positions are not fixed, but the center is usually the tallest player and takes a position close to the opponents' basket; the forwards are stationed to the sides of the center, along the end lines or farther out on the wings; and the guards (usually smaller and quicker than the center and forwards) play a defensive role. Teams also have several substitute players who are brought into the game to give the other players a rest or to take advantage of their own special abilities.

The game begins with a "jump ball" at the center of the court. The referee tosses the ball in the air between two opposing

Basketballs must bounce 3 ft. 11 in.– 4 ft. 6½in. (1.19– 1.38m) when dropped onto a solid floor from a height of 5 ft. 10 in. (1.78m).

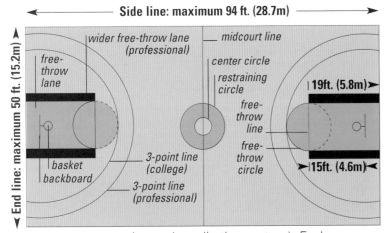

Side line: maximum 94 ft. (28.7m)

wider free-throw lane (professional)

midcourt line

center circle

restraining circle

free-throw lane

free-throw line

19ft. (5.8m)

free-throw circle

15ft. (4.6m)

End line: maximum 50 ft. (15.2m)

3-point line (college)

3-point line (professional)

basket
backboard

Diagram of a basketball court. The dimensions may vary slightly.

players (usually the centers). Each one jumps up and tries to tap the ball to a teammate. Players may not hold, push, slap, or trip an opponent. Such violations are called personal fouls, for which free throws are given from the free-throw line. If a player commits five personal fouls (six in professional competitions), he or she is disqualified from the game and replaced by a substitute.

If the ball goes off the court, or out-of-bounds, the team that was not the last to touch it throws the ball into play again. There are time limits set on how long a player can hold the ball, how long an offensive player can stay inside the free-throw lane, and how long a team can be in possession of the ball.

Michael Jordan of the Chicago Bulls goes for the hoop.

SEE ALSO:
Sports

A field goal is a basket made from the court during normal play and scores two points. Three points are counted for a field goal shot from beyond the three-point line (22 ft. or 19 ft. from the basket). A goal from a free throw counts one point. The team that scores more points in the specified amount of time wins the game.

High school basketball games are played in four 8-minute quarters, while younger teams play four 6-minute quarters. College games are divided into two 20-minute halves, professional games into four 12-minute quarters. In the second half of the game the teams "trade" ends,

DID YOU KNOW?

The metal rim of the basket should be exactly 10 ft. (3m) above the floor. It is 18 in. (45.7cm) in diameter, nearly wide enough to fit two basketballs at the same time. It is attached to a backboard that can be rectangular or circular. A large rectangle is painted on the backboard to help a player aim when trying to bounce the ball off the backboard and into the basket.

A regulation basketball is 30 in. (76.2cm) in circumference and weighs from 20 to 22 oz. (567 to 624g). The surface of the ball is made of orange or brown leather or rubber, with a dimpled surface. The ball is inflated with air so that it bounces easily.

and each then shoots for the basket it defended in the first half. Teams may call a time-out (a short rest period) at any time, when substitutes may be brought on.

Conferences

The National Basketball Association (NBA) now has 29 teams (28 in U.S. cities and one in Canada) divided into the Eastern and Western Conferences. Each team normally plays 82 games in a season. At the end of the regular season the top 16 teams compete in a series of playoffs to determine the NBA champion. The Women's National Basketball Association (WNBA) was founded in 1997.

✳ BAT

Bats are the only mammals that fly through the air with wings. Flying squirrels and flying lemurs do not fly; they just glide from tree to tree.

Bats are found in almost every part of the world except the polar regions. Most bats live in large groups called colonies. Many eat insects, others eat fruit or nectar, and a few eat fish or meat, while vampire bats feed on blood. Nearly all bats are nocturnal (active at night).

The Australian flying fox is one of nearly 1,000 species of bats in the world today—this represents almost a quarter of all mammal species.

Finding their way

A bat's wing is not like a bird's wing. A bird's wing is formed chiefly of feathers, but a bat's wing is a double layer of skin stretched over the thin bones of its "arm" and "fingers," and linked to its legs. Because they fly at night, bats have to use a kind of radar to find their way around. Each bat sends out ultrasonic sounds (sounds that are too high for people to hear). When the sound waves hit an object, they bounce back, and the bat picks up the echo with its relatively large ears. This means that bats can avoid each other and obstacles such as trees, and track the insects that they feed on.

Endangered animals

Many species of bat are dropping in numbers. There are various reasons for this. In Europe superstitions about bloodsucking have made people fear bats, and as a result many of the animals have been needlessly killed. In Africa and parts of Asia flying foxes, a fruit-eating species of bat, are killed for food. Bats also suffer because the trees where they roost have been destroyed. In many parts of the world today special efforts are being made to help threatened bats.

AMAZING FACTS !

The smallest species of bat (and the smallest mammal) is Kitti's hog-nosed bat. It weighs $\frac{1}{10}$ oz. (1.5g) and has a 6-in. (15cm) wingspan.
The largest species of bat is the flying fox, which weighs 3 lb. (1.5kg) and has a 6-ft. (2m) wingspan.
The Mexican free-tailed bat population of Texas eats about 20,000 tons of insects a year.
Vampire bats (below) from South and Central America feed on the blood of cattle and other mammals.

SEE ALSO:
Animal;
Mammal;
Radar &
Sonar

＊BEAR

Most bears live in forests in mountain regions. They feed mainly on the meat of other mammals, but also eat plants and sometimes fish.

SEE ALSO:
Animal;
Camouflage;
Carnivore;
Hibernation;
Mammal

Bears, including the American black bear and the grizzly bear (a type of brown bear), have powerful legs and long, sharp claws that they use for climbing trees. Their thick fur protects them against cold winters in their mountain homes.

Bears spend much of the day feeding: They need lots of leaves, nuts, and berries to fuel their huge bodies. Some bears are good at fishing, catching salmon as they swim up streams toward their breeding grounds. Bears also chase small mammals, such as young deer.

Bears are aggressive animals. Male bears fight each other over females. She-bears are at their most dangerous when they are rearing their young: If they think their cubs are threatened, they may attack other bears and even people.

Although bears are rather ungainly when they move on land, they are extremely agile when climbing trees. ▼

AMAZING FACTS!

Kodiak bears are the world's largest carnivores (meat eaters). They live on Kodiak Island, Alaska, and on the neighboring mainland. Males are up to 9 ft. (2.8m) long and weigh up to 1,700 lb. (780kg).

Bears generally live alone, except during the breeding season.

In winter bears fall into a deep sleep that is like hibernation; but their body temperature does not drop, and they still have their normal bodily functions.

Polar bears have thick fur on the soles of their feet to help them grip ice.

Other bears

Polar bears live in the northern Arctic around the North Pole. They have almost white fur that camouflages them against the ice and snow. They feed mainly on seals and young walrus, which they catch either by stalking at the ocean's edge or by waiting beside holes in the ice where sea mammals come up for air. They also eat fish and, in the summer, grass and herbs. Polar bears are strong swimmers.

Other bears include the Himalayan black bear, which has a mane of thick fur; the insect-eating sloth bear of India and Sri Lanka; and the small, short-haired Malayan sun bear. Most bears live in the northern hemisphere. The one exception is the spectacled bear, which lives in the Andes Mountains of South America.

● *Look in the Index for:* ＊BEATLES, THE

BEETHOVEN, LUDWIG VAN (1770–1827)

Beethoven was one of the greatest composers of classical music. His achievement is even more amazing because for much of his life he was deaf.

Beethoven was born in 1770 in Bonn, Germany. His father was an alcoholic and wanted his son to earn money by performing. Young Ludwig was often dragged out of bed at night and made to practice the piano. By the age of 13 he was already working as an organist. After his mother died, when he was 18, Beethoven had to take charge of the family. He played for many princes in and around Vienna, Austria.

Then, about 1799, Beethoven discovered that he was going deaf. After this he developed a new musical style that reflected his violent emotions. At about this time Beethoven composed the Fifth Symphony, one of the most popular and influential of all his works. By 1820 he was so deaf that he could communicate with other people only in writing. But this was his most creative period, during which he wrote his greatest works: the last five piano sonatas, the Mass in D (*Missa solemnis*), the Ninth Symphony, and the last five string quartets.

In 1826 his nephew Karl tried to commit suicide. This badly affected Beethoven's health. He died on March 26, 1827.

Ludwig van Beethoven in his late thirties.

SEE ALSO:
Composers;
Music

BELARUS see **EUROPE, CENTRAL & EASTERN**

BELGIUM see **NETHERLANDS, BELGIUM, & LUXEMBOURG**

BELIZE see **AMERICA, CENTRAL**

BENIN see **AFRICA, WEST**

BHUTAN see **ASIA**

BIBLE

The Bible is a collection of books that forms the basis of the beliefs and laws of two religions, Judaism and Christianity.

The Christian Bible is divided into two parts: the Old Testament (39 books, originally in Hebrew, about events before the birth of Jesus Christ) and the New Testament (27 books, originally in Greek, about Jesus). The Jews use the Hebrew Bible, which is almost the same as the Old Testament. The Torah (the first five books) sets out the laws of Judaism.

Pope John Paul II raises a copy of the Bible during Mass in Israel.

Look in the Index for: **BELL, ALEXANDER GRAHAM**

Before printing, the Bible was copied by hand. This illuminated (highly illustrated) version dates from the 1200s.

The books of the Bible are the work of many different writers. They include religious laws, stories to illustrate how people should lead their lives, and songs of praise called psalms. There are also history books. Some stories, such as those of Adam and Eve, Noah and the flood, and Abraham, the founder of Judaism, are also found in the Koran, the sacred writings of Islam. The books of the Hebrew Bible were handed down by word of mouth for hundreds of years, but the books of the New Testament were written soon after the events they describe.

Translations

The Christian Bible was soon translated into Latin, which was the most widely known language at the time. In the 1500s the Christians in western Europe were divided into Roman Catholics and Protestants by a dispute called the Reformation. A German translation of the Bible by Martin Luther (a Protestant) set the pattern for many later versions in other languages. In England reformers translated the Bible into English so that everyone could read it. In 1611 a bible in English (known as the King James Version) became the standard English text. It is still used today. The first American English version of the Bible was published in 1901. Jews still read the Hebrew version of the Bible.

DID YOU KNOW?

The word *bible* comes from the Greek *biblion*, meaning book. The first four books of the New Testament—Matthew, Mark, Luke, and John—tell the story of the life of Jesus and are called the Gospels: This word comes from Old English and means "good news." Some versions of the Bible include extra books, called the Apocrypha.

SEE ALSO: Christianity; Islam; Judaism; Reformation

✳ BIBLIOGRAPHY

A bibliography is a list of books and other writing at the end of a book or report. It tells you where the author found the information for his or her work.

When you write a school project or report, or when an author writes a book, it is important to tell the reader where the information came from. Then the reader can decide how accurate the research is, how much of the work is based on the author's own ideas, and how much came from other books and articles.

Bibliographies give all the information about a book in a particular order. First comes the author's last name, followed by the first name, or initials. Put a period after the name. Then write the name of the book. If you are using a computer to write the report, you should put the title of books in italics. Put a period after the title, and then include the information about the book itself: where it was published, the name of the publisher, and the date it was published. List all the books in alphabetical order of the authors.

If you also read articles for the research, include them as well. Start with the name of the author (or the publishing company if a separate author is not listed). The title of the article should go in quotation marks. The title of the magazine should go in italics, followed by the volume number,

Book title   Article title

Author
Publisher details
Publisher (no author)

Series title

CD-ROM title
Publisher details

Website name

Internet address

Magazine title

Volume number
and title

Books and Articles
Sparrow, Giles. *Exploring The Solar System: Moon.*
Chicago: Heinemann Library, 2001.
Cobblestone Publishing. "To the Moon" *Odyssey* (April 1999): 22–24.

Reference Works
Inventors and Inventions, Vol. 1: *Air and Space.*
Danbury, CT: Grolier, 2000.
Space Encyclopedia. London: Dorling Kindersley, 1999.

CD-ROM
Eyewitness Encyclopedia of Space and the Universe. London: Dorling
Kindersley, 1998.

Websites
National Aeronautics and Space Administration (NASA)
http://www.nasa.gov.

New Book of Knowledge, Grolier Online
http://go.scholasticlibrary.com.

issue number, date of publication (in parentheses), and page number. You may have found information in an encyclopedia, on a CD-ROM, or on a website on the Internet. These sources should also be included in a bibliography. Encyclopedias and CD-ROMs should be listed according to title, followed by the place they were published, the name of the publisher, and the date of publication. If you list a website, give its name (in bold letters if you are using a computer), followed by the complete web address on a separate line.

SEE ALSO:
Book; Book
Report

✳ BICYCLE AND MOTORCYCLE

All bicycles and motorcycles have two wheels. Bicycles are propelled by their riders; motorcycles have engines.

A German inventor, Karl von Drais, was the first person to build a bicycle. It was made of wood and named a running machine (*Laufmaschine*) because the rider had to stride along to make the cycle work. It was only really useful for downhill runs. It was followed in the 1870s by the Ordinary, or penny-farthing (named for the largest and smallest British coins of the time). This cycle had a tiny rear wheel and a huge front wheel, with pedals attached to the hub. Finally, in 1885 John Kemp Starley came up with the Rover Safety, a bicycle with a chain that linked the pedals to the rear wheel. The design has since been modified and improved to produce the bicycles we know today.

There are modern bicycles for many different purposes: touring bikes, mountain or trail bikes, and racing bikes. The most advanced racing bikes have lightweight, carbon-fiber frames and wheel spokes that are enclosed to reduce drag from the air.

A typical modern bicycle. The rider's gloves, helmet, and sunglasses are for protection.

Very narrow, high pressure tires reduce friction as the cyclist races along; even the helmet and clothes the cyclist wears are designed to reduce wind resistance. The recumbent bike is a relatively new idea: The rider lies back in a seat, with his or her feet on pedals in front that drive a long chain attached to the rear wheels.

Motorcycles

The first motorcycle to appear in public had a gasoline engine attached to a wooden-framed bicycle. It was built in 1885 by Gottlieb Daimler, a German who later became famous as a manufacturer of cars. Today's motorcycles are often as powerful as cars. Usually, riders control the throttle and the front-wheel brake through controls on the handlebars. A foot pedal controls the rear-wheel brake.

SEE ALSO: Leonardo da Vinci; Transportation

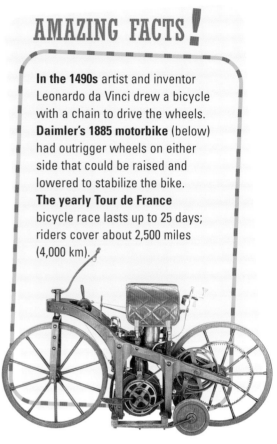

AMAZING FACTS!

In the 1490s artist and inventor Leonardo da Vinci drew a bicycle with a chain to drive the wheels. **Daimler's 1885 motorbike** (below) had outrigger wheels on either side that could be raised and lowered to stabilize the bike. **The yearly Tour de France** bicycle race lasts up to 25 days; riders cover about 2,500 miles (4,000 km).

✳ BILL OF RIGHTS

On December 15, 1791, the Bill of Rights added 10 amendments to the Constitution to set out the basic rights of citizens.

The right to trial by jury is one of the many basic human freedoms protected by the Bill of Rights.

James Madison, the "Father of the Constitution," took the lead in the First Congress in pressing for the Bill of Rights.

The bill's 10 amendments

The first eight amendments set forth specific guarantees and liberties. The Ninth Amendment acknowledges that the American people have rights that are not specified in the Constitution or the Bill of Rights. The 10th Amendment emphasizes the national character of the constitutional system.

The First Amendment guarantees freedoms of religion, speech, and the press, as well as the right to assemble and to petition a government.

The Second Amendment notes the need for a "well regulated militia" (a body of citizen soldiers called to serve during times of emergency or war) and declares that the people's right "to keep and bear arms shall not be infringed."

The Third Amendment prevents the government from making citizens shelter soldiers in their homes.

The Fourth Amendment protects individuals from unreasonable searches and seizures (either of themselves or of their property and possessions) by law-enforcement officials.

The Fifth Amendment stops someone being tried twice for the same crime. It states that people cannot be forced to give evidence against themselves. It also states that people accused of a crime must be properly notified of the charges and given a fair hearing.

The Sixth Amendment establishes the right of an accused person to a public trial by jury. The accused also has the right to have a lawyer.

The Seventh Amendment ensures trial by jury in civil suits.

The Eighth Amendment bans "cruel and unusual punishments" (either mental or physical) of those convicted of a crime.

State and national courts enforce the Bill of Rights. The Supreme Court has the final word in determining whether or not the principles contained in the Bill of Rights have been violated.

SEE ALSO: Constitution; Government, U.S.; Madison, James; Revolution, American; Supreme Court

BIOGRAPHY AND AUTOBIOGRAPHY

Writing about individual lives is an old practice. The Bible is full of stories about the prophets and saints. The earliest ancient Greek biographer was Xenophon, who wrote about the philosopher Socrates in the fourth century B.C. The best-known Latin biographer is Suetonius, author of *Lives of the Caesars* in A.D. 120.

Modern biographers' aims are varied. Some wish to tell an exciting, dramatic, and often inspirational human story. Others study the life of a person so that readers can benefit from the subject's experience and thus learn more about the world and life in general. Another type of biographer tries to bring the past back to life by describing the impact of a distinguished individual on his or her times.

A biography may take years to write. It may require thousands of hours of study in libraries, law courts, city halls, museums, and family archives. Frequently biographers must travel many miles to visit the places where their subjects lived and worked, and interview people still alive who can add to the body of knowledge. Often the search is

Actress and singer Cher with her 1998 autobiography.

11

An Internet biography of King Hussein of Jordan (1935–99).

SEE ALSO: Bible; Greece, Ancient; Roman Empire

frustrating. A researcher is a kind of detective who hunts down clues and puts together scraps of evidence.

Biographers have to be objective and tell the complete truth based on their findings and not conceal the subject's faults or allow their own opinions to take over. A good biographer becomes at one with the person he or she writes about.

Autobiography

Auto comes from the Greek for "self," or "one's own." Sometimes an autobiography is ghostwritten, that is, written by someone else, frequently a person with journalistic experience. Sometimes the real writer is completely unknown. Successful autobiography is not as easy as it might seem. The best life stories inspire the reader with their honesty, but others are written to get money, attention, sympathy, or revenge.

✳ BIOLOGY

Biology is the scientific study of organisms, or living things—the way they work, their structure, and their interrelationships.

Ecology is a branch of biology. Here ecologists test the biological health of Thighman Lake, Mississippi, by taking samples of bottom sediments.

It is easy to say that biology is the scientific study of living things, but how do we know what is living and what is not? To answer this question, biologists have figured out a set of characteristics that are shared by all organisms.

All living things are made of cells. Most cells are so small that they can be seen only under a microscope. Some organisms, such as bacteria, consist of just one cell. Others might have billions.

All organisms need energy to stay alive. Animals get energy from food. Green plants and some small organisms get energy from the sun through a process called photosynthesis.

Organisms grow as they get older. They become larger and change shape. Organisms create new individuals of the same type to replace those that die. This

FAMOUS BIOLOGISTS

The following are some of the most influential biologists in history.

Hippocrates
(about 460–377 B.C.)
Ancient Greek physician who introduced scientific methods to medicine.

Harvey, William (right)
(1578–1657)
English physician who described the circulation of blood in the body.

Van Leeuwenhoek, Antonie
(below right) (1632–1723)
Dutch naturalist who made many discoveries with a microscope.

Carolus Linnaeus (von Linné, Carl) (1707–78)
Swedish botanist who classified the living world, giving each plant and animal its own scientific name.

Schleiden, Matthias (Jakob) (1804–81),
and **Schwann, Theodor (Ambrose Hubert)**
(1810–82)
German scientists who developed cell theory.

Darwin, Charles (Robert)
(1809–82)
English naturalist whose theory of evolution changed people's view of the world.

Mendel, Gregor (Johann) (1822–84)
Austrian monk and botanist who developed the theory of heredity and genetics.

is called reproduction. Life is self-perpetuating—in other words, it can come only from other living things.

Evolution

Organisms can sense and respond to changes in their world. In order to survive, an organism must adjust, or adapt, to such changes. As winter sets in, for example, the fur of an arctic fox turns white and thick to keep it warm and make it less noticeable against the snow. The organisms that adapt best to changes in the environment are most likely to survive and reproduce. This process explains why organisms change, or evolve, over time.

Biologists at work

Biology is divided into many different fields. People who specialize in studying plants are called botanists. Those who concentrate on animals are zoologists. Some zoologists specialize in specific animals. Ornithologists study birds, and marine biologists study animals that live in the oceans and seas. Some biologists study particular parts of organisms. Biochemists study chemical reactions in organisms; geneticists study genes, which determine the qualities organisms inherit from their parents. Ecologists study how living organisms relate to each other within their environment.

In the post-September 11, 2001, war against terrorism a biologist analyzes samples taken from a suspect letter for traces of the deadly anthrax bacteria.

SEE ALSO: Animal; Biome; Botany; Camouflage; Cell; Circulatory System; Ecology; Evolution; Genetics; Plant; Reproduction; Scientific Instruments; Zoology

✳ BIOME
Biome is the scientific term for a community of specific types of plants and animals that covers a large area of the earth's surface.

The type of biome is usually determined by the type of climate in that region. The major land biomes are grasslands (known as prairies in North America, savannas in Africa, steppes in Asia, and pampas in South America), deserts, chaparral, deciduous forests, coniferous forests, tundra, and tropical rainforests. Aquatic biomes exist in rivers, lakes, and oceans.

Most of the different kinds of biomes can be found on every continent except Antarctica. Each place has unique species of plants and animals, yet the plants and animals of a particular biome tend to be similar regardless of where they are in the world. For example, spine-covered cacti are common in the southwestern deserts of the United States. In African deserts similar prickly plants called euphorbs grow in abundance. Both have adapted similarly to living in the hot, dry desert biome.

In many parts of the world nature's biomes have been altered by people. In the dry grasslands of the Sahel, in western Africa, for example, domestic goats and sheep have overgrazed the land. The thin layer of topsoil has been blown away, and the Sahel is becoming a desert. This process, called desertification, also threatens other parts of the world.

People in Central America, South America, and Southeast Asia have been burning down the tropical rainforests to make farmland and cutting down the trees for lumber. Each year millions of acres of rainforest are destroyed. Their loss may seriously change the world's climate. Environmental groups and government agencies are working to protect the world's biomes. In this way the earth's precious natural resources can be preserved for future life.

One of the biggest threats to biomes is the action of humans. Here a part of the Amazon rainforest in Brazil is burned down to create space for an enlarged cattle ranch.
▼

A prairie in Wyoming. Land such as this is part of the earth's grassland biome.

Grasslands

Grasslands are a biome in which the average annual rainfall is 10–40 in. (254–1,016mm). Animals include large herds of grazing animals, such as zebras and gazelles, and predators, such as lions, leopards, and hyenas.

Deserts

A desert is a biome in which there is less than 10 in. (254mm) of annual rain. The days are very hot, and the nights are cold. Succulents, plants that store water in their leaves or stems, are among the major plants. Many animals stay underground during the day and come out at night. Some can survive with very little water.

Chaparral

Chaparrals are dense growths of shrubs and trees. They are found on the coasts of the Mediterranean Sea, southern California, central Chile, the southern tip of Africa, and southern Australia. Some areas average as little as 10 in. (254mm) of rain a year, all of which falls in winter. Warm, moist air from the oceans prevents conditions from being as severe as those in the desert. The main plants are tough evergreen shrubs with small leathery leaves. Most of the animals there are adapted to a dry climate.

Deciduous forests

The forests of eastern North America, Central Europe, eastern China, and the southeast coast of Australia are made up of deciduous trees, or trees that grow and shed their leaves in a seasonal pattern. Rain falls year-round, averaging about 40 in. (1,016mm). Many plants and animals flourish, including ferns, mosses, fungi, insects, songbirds, amphibians, deer, and small mammals.

Coniferous forests

Temperate coniferous forest is found in moist, coastal environments, including the northern Pacific coast of North America and the east coast of Australia. In California these forests contain giant sequoia (also called redwoods); in Australia they feature towering eucalyptus trees. Boreal forests stretch across the northern reaches of North America, Europe, and Asia. Pine, spruce, and firs are the most common trees. Many different types of animal live there, especially in the summer. They include moose, elk, deer, migratory birds, and bears.

The beautiful fall colors of a deciduous forest in Maine.

Tundra

North of the boreal forest lies the treeless tundra. Beneath it is a layer of frozen ground called permafrost, which may be

For a few short weeks in the summer in Alaska even the Arctic is green.

over 1,000 ft. (305m) thick. The soil on top of the permafrost thaws for only eight weeks during the short Arctic summer. The small flowering plants and dwarf trees that live here have to grow, bloom, and set seed quickly to survive. In summer the tundra teems with life—there are herds of caribou and reindeer,

and flocks of migrating birds feeding on the numerous insects. As summer fades, many mammals travel to the forests, and the birds fly south.

Tropical rainforests
In these biomes around the equator annual rainfall averages between 80 and 200 in. (2,000–5,000mm), and falls evenly year-round. Temperatures hardly vary, hovering just below 80°F (27°C) day and night. This steady environment has the greatest variety of plant, animal, and insect species of all the biomes, ranging from parrots to monkeys and jaguars.

SEE ALSO: Arctic; Conservation; Desert; Ecology; Forest; Grassland; Habitat; Rainforest; Ocean & Sea

* BIRD
Birds are found in every area of the world—there are more than 9,000 species. Although most birds can fly, a few have evolved into flightless creatures.

The fossilized remains of an Archaeopteryx, thought to be the earliest species of bird.

Other animals have wings and can fly, but no other creature is covered with feathers. Feathers are formed in special skin cells from a protein called keratin. Feathers smooth and streamline the bird's body, enabling it to move easily through the air or water; they also protect its skin and help it maintain its body temperature.

There are three basic types of flight: flapping, gliding, and soaring. Most birds use flapping flight—that is, after they take off, they continue to fly by moving their wings up and down. When gliding, birds keep their wings extended and coast downward. During soaring flight birds use the energy of rising columns of warm air, called thermals, to fly without having to flap their wings.

Skeleton and muscles
The body systems of birds are all adapted to flight. Over time the skeleton of the bird has developed into an airy, lightweight, yet strong frame. Birds have a large breastbone, or sternum, that protects their internal organs and provides them with strong support for the attached muscles that power flight.

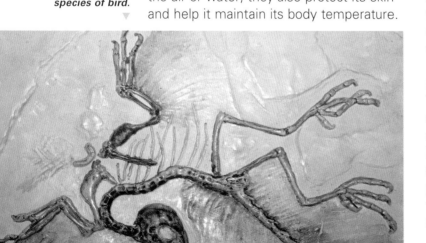

Like all birds of prey, the red-tailed hawk has a powerful, hooked bill and sharp talons for seizing its victims and tearing them to pieces.

The largest muscles in a bird are the pectoral (breast) muscles. They may account for as much as one-fifth of a bird's entire weight. They are attached to the long bone of the wing. When they contract during flight, the bird's wings are pulled down. Other, smaller muscles contract during flight to pull the wings up.

Feeding

Birds feed on a wide variety of food—from fruit and seeds to dead animals. Their beaks are adapted to suit their diet. An eagle, for example, has a powerful, hooked bill to tear its prey to bits.

Because birds have no teeth, their digestive systems must grind up food so that the energy stored in it can be used. Some birds have a gullet storage pouch called a crop. It allows a bird to feed quickly and digest its meal later in safety.

Nearly all birds have a stomach made up of two parts. The first part secretes strong digestive juices. The second part, called the gizzard, has muscular walls that grind and pulverize food. Birds often swallow small pebbles and grit to aid the grinding.

Birds have a higher body temperature, a faster heart rate, and a greater need for oxygen than mammals, so they must eat a great deal of food to get the energy they need to fuel their bodies.

When flying, birds require 10 to 20 times more oxygen than they need when they are at rest. To get the extra oxygen, birds increase their rate of breathing.

Senses

As a group, birds have the best vision of all animals. Their large eyes, which sometimes weigh more than their brains, provide keen sight and often excellent color perception. Hearing is also well developed in birds, with some night birds having especially acute awareness of sound. Only a few birds, such as the kiwi, have a highly developed sense of smell. The kiwi is nearly blind and relies on its sense of smell to find food.

Communicating

Bird songs may sound beautiful, but birds do not sing to make music. They sing to attract mates and to tell other birds to stay off their territory (an area they consider theirs). Birds generally have between 5 and 14 songs, but some species have many more. Subtle differences in the pitch and timing of the songs distinguish individual birds.

Reproduction

All birds lay eggs and care for them in one way or another. The place where birds lay their eggs is called a nest. Some birds lay eggs on bare cliff ledges; others build elaborate structures to hold the eggs.

Eight or nine out of every ten birds die during their first year. For

The great horned owl has large eyes that enable it to see well in the dark and detect even the slightest movement at great distances.

Ducks are birds that live on and near water.

SEE ALSO:
Animal;
Conservation;
Dinosaur;
Endangered
Species;
Fossil;
Migration

The bald eagle hunts for fish along the rivers and lakes of North America.

most species the greatest threats are bad weather and predators. Regardless of their regular diet, the adults feed their young foods rich in proteins. Before long the nest becomes overcrowded. It is time for the baby birds to leave the nest; this is called fledging.

The migration cycle

Some birds remain in the same area all their lives and are known as residents. Billions of birds travel to distant places: They are called migrants. In the Northern Hemisphere resident birds face long, cold winters and scarce food supplies. It is easier for them to survive in warmer southern countries, even though many migrating birds are killed by storms and other hazards. Birds return north to breed because there are fewer predators there, as well as an extremely large supply of insects to feed growing young.

History of birds

Most scientists now believe that birds evolved from small two-legged dinosaurs called theropods.

The earliest known bird is *Archaeopteryx*, which lived about 150 million years ago. It was about the size of a blue jay and had wings and feathers. Unlike modern birds, it also had a long, bony tail and teeth. The bone structure of its legs suggests that it was a good runner, and scientists believe *Archaeopteryx* could fly, but not very well.

Bird populations have been drastically reduced by people who have hunted them for their meat and feathers. Another threat is the popularity of birds, especially parrots, as pets. This has led to many birds being caught and caged. Many birds have also died when their habitats were destroyed, as woods and forests were cut down, marshes drained, and swamps filled to provide land for farming, development, and grazing. Birds have also suffered from the introduction into new lands of predators, such as cats and rats.

AMAZING FACTS!

The Cuban bee hummingbird is the smallest living bird. It weighs about 1/20 oz. (1.6g) and is about 2 in. (5cm) long. It moves its wings 70 times a second when flying and hovering in front of flowers.

The ostrich lays a gigantic egg that can weigh up to 4 lb. (1kg). The tiny Cuban bee hummingbird's egg is only 1/4 in. (5mm) long and weighs 1/100 oz. (.25g). More than 5,000 hummingbird eggs would fit inside an ostrich egg.

The nest built by the male dusky scrub fowl of Australia is a gigantic mound of rotting leaves, sticks, and grass that can sometimes measure 36 ft. (11m) across and over 16ft. (5m) high.

The feather cloak of the Hawaiian King Kamehameha I took at least a hundred years to make and used about 450,000 feathers from more than 80,000 birds.

✳ BLACK DEATH

The Black Death was a plague (disease) that swept through Europe in the mid–1300s. It killed nearly a third of the continent's total population.

The symptoms of the most common form of the plague were headaches, aching joints, fever, and vomiting. In the bubonic form of the disease victims developed dark patches on their bodies, and their tongues turned black. This is how the Black Death got its name. Victims usually died in three days. The plague was caused by bacteria carried by a flea that traveled on rats. It spread to humans and animals through bites from infected fleas.

The plague came to Europe from Asia through the Black Sea port of Kaffa (modern Feodosiya) in the Crimea. Traders working there in 1347 became infected and took the disease to Italy. From there it spread rapidly, reaching Scotland and Scandinavia by 1350.

Burying victims of the Black Death in Tournai, Belgium.

No one understood how the disease spread. People used incense, aromatic oils, and even church bells to try to rid the air of infection. In many cities Jews were blamed and killed or driven out. Many Jews fled to Poland, a country that largely escaped the effects of the plague. About 25 million people died in Europe.

SEE ALSO:
Disease;
Middle
Ages

✳ BLACK HOLE

Black holes are places in outer space where the force of gravity is so strong that matter and energy (including light) are sucked in and cannot escape.

Gravity is the force that attracts all the objects in the universe to each other: It makes a ball fall to the ground if you throw it in the air, and it keeps the earth orbiting around the sun. Black holes form when a large star (many times bigger than the sun) dies. Over billions of years stars start to cool. Their gravity then makes them collapse under their own weight. As dying stars get smaller and smaller, their gravity gets stronger and stronger. Any matter or energy attracted inward by this force cannot escape.

Black holes are invisible, but they can be detected when they are close to other stars. That is because they suck gas from neighboring stars. Gas that is about to be sucked into the black hole throws out x-rays that can be detected by scientific instruments on earth.

An artist's impression of a black hole at the center of a swirling whirlpool of hot gas.

SEE ALSO:
Gravity; Star

*BLACKWELL, ELIZABETH (1821–1910)

Elizabeth Blackwell was the first woman doctor in the United States. She was born in Bristol, England, but in 1832 her family emigrated.

A drawing of Elizabeth Blackwell in middle age.

Blackwell started work as a teacher and then applied to medical school. Most schools turned her down, but she was accepted by the Geneva Medical College, New York. She graduated in 1849.

Because Blackwell was a woman, most hospitals would not let her practice medicine, so in 1853 she set up a clinic for the poor in New York City. She later set up the New York Infirmary for Women and Children, which was staffed almost entirely by women. In 1868 the Infirmary expanded to include the Women's Medical College.

In 1869 Blackwell returned to England, where she helped found the London School of Medicine for Women. She died on May 31, 1910, at the age of 89.

*BLOOD

Blood is like a river of life flowing through your body. It carries food to the cells, takes waste away from them, and helps defend you against disease.

A woman gives blood to help others who have lost their own. Doctors must ensure that donors and recipients have matching groups.

The heart pumps blood to the lungs and through the arteries (tubes carrying blood away from the heart). From there blood circulates to every part of the body. More than half the blood in the human body is plasma, a liquid that can carry dissolved chemicals around the body. There are three types of solid carried in the plasma: red cells, white cells, and platelets.

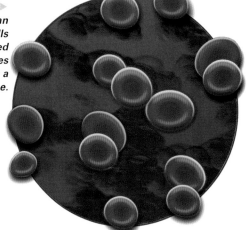

Red human blood cells magnified 450 times under a microscope.

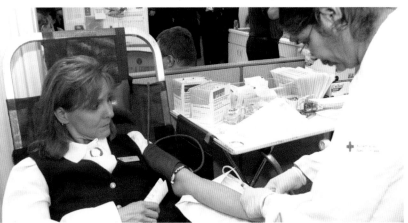

There are more red blood cells in the body than any other kind of cell. They pick up oxygen from the air that is breathed into the lungs and carry it to the cells that need oxygen to work. White blood cells fight against tiny microbes, called viruses and bacteria, that cause disease. They create proteins called antibodies, which can make the microbes harmless. The

---

● *Look in the Index for:* *BLIZZARD

platelets form a jellylike substance that makes blood clot, so that you do not bleed to death if you cut yourself.

Blood groups

Everyone has similar red blood cells, but on the outside of the cells there are molecules called antigens. If you have a transfusion of blood from someone with different antigens, your blood may make the cells in the blood you have been given clump together and block your arteries and veins. There are four basic groups: group A (with A antigens), group B (B antigens), group AB (A and B antigens), and group O (neither A nor B antigens). Another set of antigens divides people into two types, Rhesus positive (Rh+) and Rhesus negative (Rh–).

SEE ALSO: Cell; Circulatory System; Digestive System; Human Body

AMAZING FACTS !

An average adult makes 200,000,000,000 blood cells every day in the bone marrow (a soft area in the middle of the bones).

If you took all the red blood cells from an average person and stacked them on top of each other, they would reach 31,000 miles (50,000km) into the sky.

Insects (right) and spiders do not have a heart to circulate blood. Instead, they have a liquid that works like blood, carrying oxygen and food around their bodies.

✳**BLUES** 👀see➤ ✳**MUSICIANS, AMERICAN**

✳**BOAT** 👀see➤ ✳**SHIP & BOAT**

✳ BOLIVIA

Bolivia lies in the heart of South America between the towering Andes Mountains and the rainforests of the Amazon River Basin.

Bolivia is one of only two countries in South America that do not have a coastline. The other is Paraguay. Bolivia's chief city, La Paz, is the world's highest capital. It stands 12,000 ft. (3,600m) above sea level.

The Andes separate Bolivia from the west coast of South America. The

▶ *Aymará musicians playing reed pipes and drums to celebrate a traditional pre-Christian Bolivian farmers' festival.*

KEY FACTS

OFFICIAL NAME
República de Bolivia

AREA
424,165 sq. mi.
(1,098,581 sq. km.)

POPULATION
8,329,000

CAPITALS
La Paz
(government);
Sucre
(constitutional)

LARGEST CITY
La Paz

MAJOR RELIGION
Roman
Catholicism

MAJOR LANGUAGES
Spanish, Quechua,
Aymará

CURRENCY:
Bolivian peso

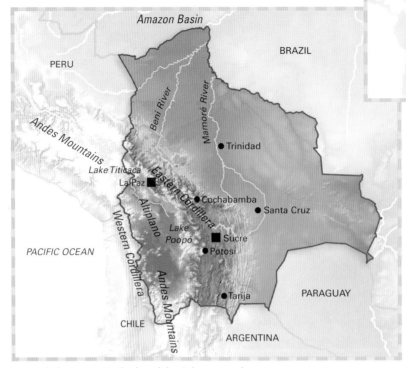

Bolivia's national flag

Bolivia was named after Simón Bolívar 1783–1830).

emerged around Lake Titicaca over 1,000 years ago, and the Quechua (pronounced ketch-wah) Indians are descended from the Inca civilization of 700 years ago. About 15 percent of the people are of Spanish descent. Spain tried to convert the Indians to Christianity, but they continue to hold traditional festivals.

mountains are at their widest here and are divided into two ranges called cordilleras. The western cordillera forms the border with Chile. Between the western and eastern cordilleras is a high plateau called the Altiplano. It is where most of the population lives, particularly around Lake Titicaca, which is the highest navigable lake in the world at 12,500 ft. (3,810m). Deep valleys in the eastern cordillera drain down to the Amazon Basin and Brazil, while in the southeast plains extend into Paraguay and Argentina.

Because of Bolivia's altitude there are great differences between day and night temperatures. However, there is little difference in temperature between summer and winter. The dry season lasts from May to November. Between December and February there are heavy rains on the Altiplano and tropical storms on the lowlands.

People

Most of the people of Bolivia are Indians. The Aymará Indians are descended from a civilization that first

Economy

Bolivia has a strong farming tradition. Most of the farms are on the Altiplano. Llamas and alpacas, long-necked animals related to camels, are native to the region, and they are used to pull carts and carry loads, as well as being kept for their valuable fur and meat.

History

The Aymará civilization was at its height between A.D. 600 and 900. In the 15th century it was conquered by the Incas, who came from the north to mine the Bolivian mountains for silver and tin. The metals attracted Spanish invaders in the 1500s. They conquered the area and ruled it until the early 1800s. The Indians, inspired by a leader named Simón Bolívar, rose up against Spanish rule, and the country declared independence in 1825. Since then Bolivia has had an unsettled history, with many different governments.

SEE ALSO: Amazon; America, South; Conquistadors; Incas

✳ BOOK

It is hard to imagine civilization without books. They are the most important way of recording and passing on information and knowledge.

Today we think of a book as a collection of paper pages with words or pictures or both printed on them, bound together in hard or soft (paperback) covers. Many copies of a book can be printed at one time to sell to bookstores and libraries.

History of books

The first books were made not from paper but from reeds called papyrus. The Egyptians were the first people to do this, from about 3500 B.C. The papyrus was rolled into scrolls, which could be sent to all parts of the Egyptian Empire. The ancient Greeks later took bookmaking a stage further by using scribes to make handwritten copies of existing scrolls.

The ancient Romans bound together thin sheets of board that had been specially treated with wax. The writing was then scratched across the surface. The Romans called a bound book a codex (from the Latin word for tree). By A.D. 400 they had found a better material—parchment. Parchment was a thin sheet of leather specially made from the skin of sheep or goats. Scribes could write on both sides

of parchment and decorate the pages with colored inks and paints. Parchment codexes soon replaced scrolls.

Invention of paper

The earliest Chinese books appeared about 5,000 years ago and were made from palm leaf or bamboo strips that were joined together at one corner and could be opened out like a fan.

Dating from A.D. *868, this Chinese woodblock is the oldest surviving printed book.*

An ancient Egyptian statue of a scribe reading a papyrus scroll.

23

In the first century A.D. the Chinese produced the world's first paper from wood chips, silk and cotton rags, hemp rope, and even old fishing nets that were made into a pulp and then molded into sheets. To start with, the Chinese wrote with special brushes, copying books by hand. From the sixth century A.D. they used carved wooden blocks to print characters on the pages.

The Chinese jealously guarded their secret method of making paper. It was not until the eighth century, when some Chinese craftsmen were taken prisoner by Arabs, that anyone else discovered how to make it. The craft did not reach Europe until the 12th century.

Books were still copied by hand until the 1400s. The invention of the printing press resulted in a huge increase in the number of books that could be made. Books also became much cheaper. Today, although methods of printing are far more advanced, the basic shape of books, bound down the left-hand side, with printing on both sides of the pages, is still the same.

SEE ALSO:
Computer;
Egypt,
Ancient;
Greece,
Ancient;
Printing;
Roman
Empire;
Writing

DID YOU KNOW?

Book production may be about to change. Soon you may no longer need to go to a bookstore or library to get a book. Some titles are already published electronically, so that you can download them onto a computer. You will have to pay a fee, and you will need special software (a computer program) to read it. Manufacturers have developed the eBook reader (below), a small hand-held computer onto which books can be downloaded and read anywhere. You can also listen to music on some readers and store other information, such as a diary or an address book.

✴ BOOK REPORT

A book report is a written analysis of a book by a reader. It should contain a summary of what the work is about and the reader's overall opinion of it.

An elementary school pupil in North Carolina presents her book report to the class.

A book report gives you (and your teacher) a record of the books you have read and what you thought about them. Book reports called reviews also appear in newspapers and magazines to tell readers about new publications or useful books on a particular topic.

When writing a book report, you should start with the author and title of the book. You will find this information on the title page and on the back of the title page. You should then explain what type of book it is: a ghost story, a tale about people in the past, an informative book about volcanoes or baseball, and so on.

The body of the report

The longest part of the report should be your description of what is in the book. When you write a report about a work of fiction, try to explain what the story is about without giving away the ending. Explain who the main characters are, where they live, and what they do. If the book is a collection of stories, explain how they are linked. For example, they may be science fiction stories or stories about children in different countries.

Next you should say how the author has put across the information. A book could be a series of letters; it may be written like a diary or like a comic book. A fact book may have lots of small

pictures with captions, or it may be nearly all text with only an occasional picture—say which kind it is.

The most important part of your report is your opinion of the book. Always explain why you did or did not like it. You may have found one of the characters was just like you or was totally unbelievable. You may be particularly interested in a fact book because it gives you further information about a subject you have already studied.

KEY POINTS

Remember to include these five pieces of information:
(1) The author, title, publisher, and date of publication
(2) The type of book
(3) What the book is about
(4) The form and style in which the book is written
(5) Your opinion of the book.

✳ BOSNIA & HERZEGOVINA ⟲ see ✳ BALKANS

✳ BOTANY

Botany is the branch of biology that studies plants, including their classification, structure, physical composition, and ecology.

Plants are essential to all life on earth. Only plants can capture the energy of the sun and use it—in a process called photosynthesis—to make food. Animals cannot do this and so depend on plants for food, as well as for the oxygen plants create during photosynthesis. Botanists have identified about 300,000 different varieties of plant, ranging in size from mosses as small as ½ in. (1cm) to redwood trees, which often are more than 295 ft. (90m) in height.

Branches of botany

There are many specialists within botany. Some botanists study plants in relation to the environment, investigating how soil and water affect their growth and development. Others study the history of plants on earth. This might involve investigating fossils and other evidence of species that became extinct thousands of years ago. This is called paleobotany.

Some botanists concentrate on particular varieties of plant. The study of

▲ **Widely known as Linnaeus, the Swedish botanist and naturalist Carl von Linné created the modern system of plant classification.**

● ***Look in the Index for:*** ✳**BOONE, DANIEL**

fungi is called mycology; the study of ferns is called pteridology. Bacteriology, the study of bacteria, is a branch of botany that is important in medicine because many diseases are caused by bacteria.

AMAZING FACTS!

The biggest ever redwood weighed more than 3,000 tons, the same as about 20 blue whales.

Apples and peaches are in the same family as roses—Rosaceae. And tomatoes are related to tobacco; they are both in the Solanum, or nightshade, family.

Other botanists study different kinds of crops or investigate extracting materials such as rubber or drugs from plants.

Plant classification

Every known variety of plant has a unique botanical name. This follows the system originally devised by the Swedish naturalist Linnaeus (1707–78) in his book *Species Plantarum*, published in 1753. Under Linnaeus's method the white pine belongs to the genus, or group, *Pinus*, and its species, or kind, is *strobus*. So the scientific name for the white pine, wherever you are in the world, is *Pinus strobus*. This method of naming botanical species is called plant taxonomy.

SEE ALSO: Biology; Disease; Drug; Ecology; Fossil; Flower; Fungi; Plant; Tree

A botanist inspects a giant senecio plant in Tanzania.

BOTSWANA see **AFRICA, SOUTHERN**

BRAIN AND NERVOUS SYSTEM

The brain controls the nerves, the spinal cord, and the sense organs (such as eyes and ears): Together, these body parts are known as the nervous system.

The brain is divided into different parts. The cerebellum controls body movement. The biggest part of the brain, the cerebrum, controls thinking, learning, memory, and imagination. The brain stem connects these parts to the spinal cord and contains the medulla, which keeps the blood flowing and the lungs breathing.

An average adult brain weighs about 3.1 lb. (1.4kg). It consists of two kinds of cell: neurons (nerve cells) and glia. Neurons send information through the body; glia clean, feed, protect, and support the neurons.

There are three main types of neuron: Sensory neurons respond to light, temperature, sound, smell, taste, and touch; motor neurons control muscles and movement; and interneurons relay information between the other two types. Most nerves are invisible to the naked eye, but some can be up to 3 ft. (1m) long.

Nervous system

The nervous system is divided into the central nervous system and the peripheral nervous system. The spinal

This magnetic resonance image (MRI) shows clearly the link between the brain and the spine. The body shape has been altered by an artist.

cord and the brain form the central nervous system. The spinal cord consists of nerves that run through the neck and back. These nerves are protected by the spinal column. The brain and spinal cord process incoming messages and send out messages to the organs and body parts on the periphery, or outside, of the body. The messages are carried by the branching network of nerves that make up the peripheral nervous system.

The spinal cord responds to some messages without involving the brain. If you touch something hot, for example, your hand recoils automatically without thinking. This is called a reflex action.

There are two main types of peripheral nerves: Sensory nerves carry messages to the central nervous system; motor nerves carry messages from the central nervous system to all parts of the body.

AREAS OF THE BRAIN

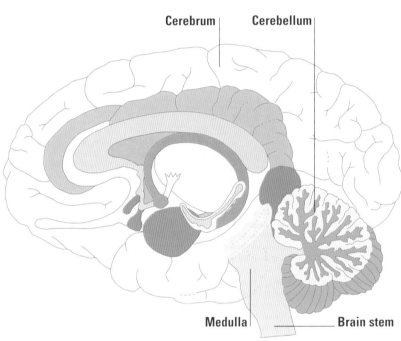

Cerebrum | Cerebellum

Medulla | Brain stem

Diagram showing the main areas of the human brain. The largest part is the cerebrum.

The autonomous nervous system is part of the peripheral nervous system. It controls vital organs such as the heart, stomach, and lungs. These nerves operate automatically, without your having to think about them.

Brain disorders

The brain is so important to the body that any damage to it can have added effects on the rest of the organism. The brain can be damaged by accident, such as a blow to the head, or by illnesses, such as epilepsy, which causes major electrical discharges within the brain.

Some people also suffer from mental illnesses, which affect their moods and thought patterns. Mental illness is not fully understood, but it can often be controlled through drugs.

SEE ALSO:
Cnidarian; Drug; Human Body

AMAZING FACTS!

The human brain accounts for just 2 percent of the body's weight, but uses up to 20 percent of the body's oxygen supply.
Scientists estimate that the human brain contains more than 100 billion neurons (nerve cells).

Other animals

In most larger animals brains and nervous systems operate in a way similar to those of humans. But single-celled organisms do not have nervous systems, and other simple animals, such as jellyfish, have a collection of nerve cells called a nerve net, but no brain.

---

*BRASS ➤ *MUSICAL INSTRUMENTS

---

*BRAZIL

Brazil is the largest country in South America. It occupies almost half the continent's area and is home to more than half its population.

Typically colorful and riotous carnival celebrations in Rio de Janeiro to mark the start of Lent.

Brazil has a mixture of hilly and low-lying areas. It is divided into five regions: the northeast, the east, the south, the central west, and the Amazon Basin. Each region contains several states.

The Amazon Basin is a vast area of rainforest, jungle, and swamp formed by the Amazon River and its tributaries. The world's largest tropical rainforest, the region is home to many rare animals.

Climate

Most of Brazil has a tropical climate—the air is moist and sticky. In parts of the Amazon Basin temperatures stay near

Brazil's national flag

KEY FACTS

OFFICIAL NAME
República
Federativa do Brazil

AREA
3,286,478 sq. mi.
(8,511,965 sq. km)

POPULATION
170,115,000

CAPITAL
Brasília

LARGEST CITY
São Paulo

MAJOR RELIGIONS
Roman Catholicism,
Evangelical
Protestantism

MAJOR LANGUAGE
Portuguese

CURRENCY
Real

95°F (35°C) all the time. Ocean breezes bring cooler weather to the Atlantic coast, and south-central Brazil has mild winters. In the far south snow occasionally falls.

Economy

Brazil is an important producer of soybeans, coffee, cacao (the source of cocoa and chocolate), sugar, corn, fruits, tobacco, and cotton. Farmers raise great herds of cattle, horses, and hogs.

Brazil is also a leading industrial nation. Many of its factories, which turn out textiles, autos, chemicals, and other products, run on hydroelectric or nuclear power. Minerals, gemstones, ores, and wood products are important exports. Tourism and other services, such as education and business, are also important to the national economy.

Major cities

Brasília is the chief city and national capital. It is a modern city laid out in the rough shape of an airplane.

São Paulo, in the state of São Paulo, is the chief industrial city of Latin America and the largest city in Brazil. It is the center of the nation's textile industry.

Rio de Janeiro, in the state of Rio de Janeiro, is one of the world's most beautiful cities, with a fine harbor, steep mountains, and wide, tree-lined avenues. Rio is host to the largest and most exciting of the carnivals (street parties) that take place before Lent every year.

The great statue of Christ the Redeemer overlooking Rio de Janeiro.

Belo Horizonte, in the state of Minas Gerais, is Brazil's third largest city. It is a major commercial and industrial area. Belém, in the state of Pará, is the main port for Amazon River shipping.

People

Most Brazilians are mestizos (people of mixed European, African, and Indian ancestry). Others have come from Japan, the Middle East, and Europe, especially Portugal. A few Indians still live in remote areas of the tropical rainforest.

Brazil has a rich cultural heritage. Its contemporary music and dance are popular all over the world. The nation's favorite sport is soccer: The national team has won the World Cup more often than any other country.

History

Brazil's earliest inhabitants were Indians. More than 100 native tribal groups inhabited the land. They did not plant crops, but hunted animals and gathered fruits and berries.

Portuguese explorers came in search of gold in 1500. Portugal then ruled Brazil for more than 300 years. Settlers brought slaves from Africa to work on plantations. Brazil became independent in 1822. In 1888 slavery was abolished. In 1889 Brazil became a republic.

Throughout the 20th century Brazil faced problems such as rebellions and falling coffee prices. The government is hard-pressed to build enough schools and hospitals for the soaring population. The rainforest is being destroyed by industry.

SEE ALSO:
Amazon;
America,
South;
Circus &
Carnival

✷ BRIDGE

Bridges carry pedestrians, cars, trains, and even canals across rivers, valleys, and canyons or between islands.

There are several types of bridge. The most basic is a beam bridge—a wooden, concrete, or metal deck (for a road or railroad to run on), supported at both ends. The first bridge was probably a fallen tree across a stream—a basic beam bridge. Beam bridges can be strengthened with trusses—triangular supports made of metal or wood.

Arched bridges

The ancient Romans discovered that they could span greater distances by building arched bridges. By the early 1800s engineers had perfected this technique.

The bridge across Sydney Harbor, Australia, is an arched structure made of concrete and steel.

Cantilever and suspension bridges

Cantilever bridges work on a principle similar to arch bridges: Two cantilevers (like projecting shelf supports) are built out toward each other from opposite sides. Each cantilever rests on a pier (solid support) and is anchored to the bank behind the pier. The cantilevers are joined in the middle by a truss.

The oldest known suspension bridges were made from ropes that were slung

The Golden Gate suspension bridge in San Francisco, California.
▼

across a gap and tied at both ends. A wooden pathway hung on shorter ropes from the two main ropes. Modern suspension bridges have brick or concrete towers, with the main cables running above them, so that the bridges can span wide rivers, straits, and estuaries.

For smaller spans cable-stay bridges are used. They are similar to suspension bridges, but the supporting cables run from the deck to the top of the tower and back down to the deck on the other side. Several towers may be used to span wide gaps.

Some bridges open to let large ships pass. There are three types: those with two sides that lift to create an opening; those that swing around on a pivot; and those with a raisable central section.

AMAZING FACTS!

The main span of the Akashi Kaikyo suspension bridge, near Kobe, Japan, is 6,529 ft. (1,990m) long.
The 23-mile (37km) Kojima-Sakaide road and rail link between Honshu and Shikoku islands, Japan, is made up of three suspension bridges and two cable-stay bridges, plus truss bridges and viaducts.
The world's longest road bridge is the 24-mile (38km) Pontchartrain Causeway across Lake Pontchartrain, Louisiana.

SEE ALSO:
Construction;
Roman
Empire

✳ BRITISH COLUMBIA

A province of Canada, British Columbia is bounded to the west by the Pacific Ocean and to the south by Idaho, Montana, and Washington.

British Columbia is the most mountainous province of Canada. The ranges include the Coast Mountains and part of the Rockies. There are many lakes, such as Atlin and Williston, and forests of huge Douglas firs. The province includes many islands in the Pacific, such as Vancouver Island and the Queen Charlotte Islands. On the Pacific coast the weather is much milder than in the rest of Canada, although the west of Vancouver Island is the wettest area of North America, receiving 100 in. (2,540mm) of rain a year.

People and history
The area now called British Columbia was inhabited for many centuries by Native Americans. In 1774 the Spanish explorer Juan Pérez became the first European known to have visited the British Columbia coast. Trade in fur flourished in the region. Gold was discovered in the Fraser River in 1858, bringing many new

settlers. In 1866 Vancouver Island and the mainland were united as the crown colony of British Columbia. British Columbia became a province of Canada in 1871.

KEY FACTS

AREA 366,255 sq. mi. (948,600 sq. km); rank, 3rd	**PROVINCE ESTABLISHED** 1871
POPULATION 4,095,900 (2001 census); rank, 3rd	**PROVINCE MOTTO** Splendor without diminishment
ELEVATION Highest—15,300 ft. (4,663m) at Mount Fairweather; Lowest—sea level	**PROVINCE FLOWER** Pacific dogwood
CAPITAL Victoria	**PROVINCE TREE** Western red cedar
ABBREVIATION BC	**PROVINCE BIRD** Steller's jay

British Columbia province flag

👀

SEE ALSO:
America,
North;
Canada

Contact with the rest of the country was improved after the completion in 1885 of the Canadian Pacific Railway between the Pacific and Atlantic coasts.

The biggest cities in British Columbia are Vancouver and Victoria in the southwest. Eighty percent of the population lives in this area of the province. British Columbia is a popular destination for immigrants from Asian countries. Major industries include forestry, mining, fishing, and tourism.

*BRUNEI see→ *ASIA, SOUTHEAST

*BUCHANAN, JAMES (1791–1868)

Despite his distinguished career, the 15th president (1857–61) is best known as the only occupant of the White House who never married.

▶ **James Buchanan in His Study,** *a painting by Charles Fenderich.*

James Buchanan was born on April 23, 1791, near Cove Gap, Pennsylvania. After graduating from Dickinson College in Carlisle, he moved to Lancaster to study law. Intelligent and hard-working, he became wealthy and popular, and came to serve Pennsylvania as a lawmaker.

From law Buchanan moved into politics, serving in the House of Representatives from 1821 to 1831. At first a member of the Federalist party, he later switched to the Jacksonian Democrats.

Foreign service
In 1832, under President Andrew Jackson, Buchanan served as U.S. minister to Russia. He helped encourage trade with that country and on his return was

elected to the Senate, where he remained until 1845, becoming chairman of the committee on foreign affairs.

Three bids for the White House
Buchanan ran for the presidency in 1844 but was beaten by James K. Polk, who appointed him secretary of state. Two years later war broke out between the United States and Mexico. Buchanan helped arrange the peace treaty in 1848 and also settled a separate quarrel with Britain over the Oregon territory.

In 1852 Buchanan ran for president a second time but was beaten again, this time by Franklin Pierce. The new president made Buchanan minister to Great Britain.

By this time the issue of slavery had divided the nation between the antislavery North and the proslavery South. A new party, the Republicans, sprang up to oppose slavery, and Buchanan's party, the Democrats, broke into two parties: North and South. Buchanan was opposed to slavery, but he managed to stay friendly with both parties. That helped him win the election in 1856, and on March 4, 1857, he became president.

In 1860–61 many Southern states seceded (broke away from) the Union. In April 1861, five weeks after Buchanan left office, the Civil War broke out. Buchanan died at home on June 1, 1868.

Could Buchanan have prevented the Civil War? Some historians say that he could have if he had been stronger, but others take the view that the war would have happened no matter who had been president.

SEE ALSO: Civil War; Slavery

KEY FACTS

BIRTHPLACE
Cove Gap, Pennsylvania

OCCUPATION
Lawyer

MARRIED
Unmarried

PARTY
Democratic

AGE WHEN PRESIDENT
65

TERM
1857–61

AGE AT DEATH
77

✳ BUDDHISM

One of the oldest religions, Buddhism is based on the teachings of a man who said he had found the cause of unhappiness and its cure.

Buddha is believed to have been an Indian prince named Siddhartha Gautama who lived 2,500 years ago. When Siddhartha was a boy, his father tried to keep him from knowing how unhappy the world really was, but he discovered sickness and death on trips outside the palace. Filled with love and pity, Siddhartha gave up his wealth, sure that this would help him understand life. After six years of failure he sat beneath a tree and vowed not to move until understanding came to him. When it did, he became known as a buddha (Sanskrit for "enlightened one"). He spent the next 45 years teaching until his death in about 483 B.C. at 80.

Beliefs
There are no gods in Buddhism. Instead, Buddhists respect and worship the Buddha and his teachings. The most important Buddhist teachings are the Four Noble Truths, which are: All is suffering; the origin of suffering is desire; suffering comes to an end in nirvana; there is a way to reach nirvana.

Buddhists believe that nirvana is a state of inner peace and understanding. Misery and suffering are caused because we desire things, people, or life itself. It is possible, however, to find inner peace (nirvana) by following Buddhism and losing our desires.

A modern Buddhist monk sounding a bell at a monastery in Bangkok, Thailand.

Buddhists believe that people die and are reborn over and over again. Those who lead a good life are reborn into a better life, while bad people suffer more the next time around. Those who lose all desire will eventually reach nirvana.

The Buddhist life

The qualities needed to lead a good life include morality, compassion, and respect for others, as well as self-discipline and wisdom. Not all Buddhists follow exactly the same rules; some are stricter than others. Some enter monasteries to escape the world's desires; many visit holy sites or public shrines to make offerings of food or flowers. In every Buddhist's life much time is spent sitting quietly and peacefully.

Today Buddhism is a major religion in Asia, but there are many Buddhists in other countries, including the United States. The best-known form of Buddhism in the West is Zen, which began in China and is now practiced mainly in Japan.

SEE ALSO: Asia; Indian Subcontinent

*BULGARIA see *BALKANS

*BURKINO FASO see *AFRICA, WEST

* BURR, AARON (1756–1836)

Aaron Burr was a hero of the American Revolution and vice president, but he later stood trial for betraying his country.

When the American Revolution started, Burr joined the army, but quit in 1779. He served in the Senate and ran for the presidency in 1800. He and Thomas Jefferson each got 73 electoral votes, but the House of Representatives chose Jefferson to be the third president, with Burr as his vice president.

Alexander Hamilton, who became secretary of the treasury, had been one of Burr's leading opponents during the campaign.

Aaron Burr at the height of his career as vice president. He was later disgraced after being arrested for treason.

The bad feeling between the men finally led to a duel on July 11, 1804. A duel is a fight (arranged in advance) with deadly weapons between two people.

Burr killed Hamilton and fled to escape a murder charge. Some people believed that Burr was planning to set up his own empire in the southwestern United States and part of Mexico. In 1807 he was arrested for treason, but a judge ruled that there was no clear proof of the crime.

After his trial Burr went to Europe, but returned to the United States in 1812. He died on Staten Island, New York, on September 14, 1836.

SEE ALSO: Hamilton, Alexander

*BURUNDI see *AFRICA, CENTRAL

✳ BUSH, GEORGE HERBERT WALKER (1924–)

George Herbert Walker Bush was born in Milton, Massachusetts, on June 12, 1924. He attended Phillips Academy in Andover. During World War II (1939–45) Bush served as a Navy torpedo bomber pilot. In 1945 he married Barbara Pierce. The Bushes had six children, one of whom,

caught lying to the country about Watergate. Bush called on Nixon to quit, which he did in August 1974.

After a period working in China, Bush returned home to be director of the Central Intelligence Agency (CIA) from 1976 to 1977. Then from 1980 to 1988 he

President George Bush poses for photographs on the rim of the Grand Canyon, Arizona.

George W. Bush, became the 43rd president of the United States in 2001.

After leaving the Navy, Bush studied economics at Yale University, then went into the oil business. He settled his family in Texas and later entered politics with the Republican Party. He was elected to the House of Representatives in 1966 and reelected in 1968, but twice ran unsuccessfully for the Senate.

In 1971 Bush was chosen to represent the United States at the United Nations, the organization for world peace and security. Two years later he was named chairman of the Republican National Committee. This was a period when President Richard M. Nixon had been

served as vice president to Ronald Reagan. In 1988 Bush himself was elected president of the United States.

The Bush administration
Americans praised President Bush for his leadership abroad. In 1989 he sent U.S. troops to capture General Manuel Noriega, dictator of Panama. When Iraq invaded Kuwait the following year, the United States led an international army in the Gulf War, forcing Iraq to withdraw.

But Bush had less success with the United States' money problems. Though he had promised not to raise taxes, he did so, and this made him unpopular. He lost the 1992 election to Bill Clinton.

SEE ALSO:

Clinton,
William;
Nixon,
Richard M.;
Reagan,
Ronald W.;
World War II

✳ BUSH, GEORGE WALKER (1946–)

George W. Bush became the 43rd president of the United States in 2001. He is the first son of a president to serve since John Quincy Adams in 1824.

KEY FACTS

BIRTHPLACE
New Haven, Connecticut

OCCUPATION
Oil executive, Major League Baseball executive, public official

MARRIED
Laura Welch

PARTY
Republican

AGE WHEN PRESIDENT
54

TERM
2001–

President George W. Bush in the White House Oval Office.

SEE ALSO:
Bush, George

George Walker Bush was born on July 6, 1946, in New Haven, Connecticut. In 1948 the Bush family moved to Texas. Bush followed in his father's footsteps, first attending Phillips Academy and then Yale University. Shortly before graduation he joined the Texas Air National Guard.

Bush spent some time supporting his father, George Bush, in politics, then entered Harvard Business School. There he earned a master's degree in business administration in 1975.

Early career and marriage

Bush went into the oil business in Texas. He founded his own oil company, Arbusto Corp., in 1977—the year in which he married Laura Welch, a librarian. In 1981 Laura gave birth to twin daughters, Jenna and Barbara.

Soon after his marriage Bush ran for the House of Representatives, but was defeated. He left the oil business and took up a political job in Washington, D.C. When Bush senior was elected president in 1988, Bush junior took on a new business venture: managing the Texas Rangers, a major league baseball team. This brought him much wealth.

From Texas to the White House

In 1994 Bush was elected governor of Texas. His support for education and for Spanish-speaking Americans made him popular, and he was reelected in 1998, making him the first Texas governor to win two consecutive four-year terms.

By now Bush had his sights set on the presidency, and he ran as the Republican candidate in the 2000 election. The race was the closest in American history. In fact, the Democratic candidate Al Gore got 500,000 more popular votes than Bush. In Florida the voting was so close that there were five weeks of recounts. Eventually it turned out that Bush had carried the state by slightly more than 500 votes. Even then, it took a Supreme Court decision to assure a Bush victory. The electoral college vote totals were 271 for Bush to 266 for Gore.

✳BUTTERFLY see ✳INSECT

● *Look in the Index for:* ✳BYRD, RICHARD E.

BYZANTINE EMPIRE

The Byzantine Empire grew out of the Roman Empire after A.D. 330, when Emperor Constantine moved his government from Rome to Byzantium.

Byzantium was an old Greek city that became known as Constantinople, for the emperor.

After Constantine died in A.D. 337, later emperors found it difficult to rule the vast Roman Empire. In 395 the empire was divided—the east was ruled from Constantinople and the west from Rome. Rome later lost most of the Western Empire (Italy, Spain, France, Britain, and northwest Africa). The eastern part survived and became known as the Byzantine Empire. Its official language was Greek. Although the Byzantines constantly had to fend off attackers, the empire lasted for centuries because its armies fought well.

Constantinople

A thousand years ago Constantinople was the largest and probably the richest city in the world. Its wealth came largely from trade. The city stood at a crossroads. All ships carrying goods between the Mediterranean Sea and the Black Sea had to pass through it. The main road from Europe to the Middle East also ran through the city. The emperors taxed all goods that came into or went out of their capital.

Byzantine culture was greatly influenced by the writings of ancient Greeks such as Plato and Aristotle.

It is because of this that ancient learning was kept alive, for Greek was not studied anywhere else at the time.

Although the Byzantine Empire was Christian, it resented the authority of the pope in Rome. Meanwhile the pope thought that the eastern emperors had too much power. Eventually the eastern and western churches divided in 1054. Churches of Byzantine origin are known today as Orthodox churches. They include the Greek Orthodox Church and the Russian Orthodox Church.

In 1204 Constantinople was sacked by Crusaders from western Europe. Civil wars and invasions further weakened the shrinking empire. In 1453, the empire ended when the Turks captured Constantinople and the last emperor was killed.

Map showing the extent of the Byzantine Empire, which grew through sea trade across the Mediterranean.

Dating from about A.D. 1000, this Byzantine mosaic depicts the Virgin Mary holding the infant Jesus.

SEE ALSO:
Christianity;
Crusades;
Greece,
Ancient;
Roman
Empire

Map labels:

ATLANTIC OCEAN — FRANCE — SPAIN — ITALY — Rome — BALKANS — GREECE — Athens — Mediterranean Sea — AFRICA — Alexandria — EGYPT — Black Sea — Constantinople — ANATOLIA — SYRIA — Damascus — PALESTINE — Jerusalem

Byzantine Empire in 554
Byzantine Empire in 1355

C

✳ CACTUS

A cactus (plural, cacti) is a plant that has adapted to very dry conditions. Cacti originated in North and South America.

Cacti grow mainly in hot, dry areas in South and Central America and the south-western United States. Some species grow as far north as Canada. People have now introduced cacti to many other parts of the world.

Cactus roots spread out close to the surface of the ground, absorbing rainwater quickly before it dries up, or evaporates. The water is stored in the stem of the plant. The outside of the cactus is thick and waxy, which keeps the water from escaping. In other plants water is lost through the holes, or pores, in the leaves, but cacti have very few pores, helping keep water in. The cactus often has spines to protect it from animals.

Cacti have spines on their surface to ward off animals that would use them as a source of food and water.

Kinds of cacti

There are around 1,500 species of cacti. The best known are the prickly pears, which have a sweet, juicy fruit and often large, colorful flowers. The biggest cactus is the saguaro, which can grow to 40 ft. (12m) tall and live for more than 200 years. Woodpeckers and desert owls often live in holes in saguaro.

Close relatives of the saguaro include the organ-pipe cactus, which looks like part of a church organ, and the night-blooming cereus. This cactus normally resembles a bundle of sticks, but white blooms appear on it for one night each year.

Desert water source

Barrel cacti can reach a height of 12 ft. (3.6m) and can be over 3 ft. (1m) in diameter. They store water in their trunks. People stranded in the desert have survived by cutting the top off the plant, pounding the pulp, and drinking the liquid that comes out. Hedgehog and pincushion cacti are small cacti that are often grown as decorative plants in gardens and homes.

AMAZING FACTS !

A species of barrel cactus called the bisnaga can grow to 9 ft. (2.7m) in height and have a diameter of 3 ft. (1m). Bisnagas this large are probably more than 1,000 years old.

SEE ALSO: Biome; Desert; Plant

Look in the Index for: ✳ CABOT, JOHN

CAESAR, JULIUS (ABOUT 100–44 B.C.)

Gaius Julius Caesar was born into a noble family and began his political career in 78 B.C. In 59 B.C. he formed an alliance with Pompey, a famous general, and Crassus, a rich nobleman. This three-man pact was called the First Triumvirate. Caesar was elected as a consul, became governor of three provinces, and successfully fought the Gauls in France and the Britons in England. Pompey later became jealous of him, and a civil war broke out between them, which Caesar won at the battle of Pharsalus in 48 B.C.

Caesar returned to Rome in 45 B.C. and was named dictator. He began many worthwhile reforms, and the following year he was appointed dictator for life. Other important Romans, such as Brutus and Cassius, thought this was too much power for one man, and they stabbed him to death in the Senate on March 15, 44 B.C.

SEE ALSO: Cleopatra; Roman Empire

Julius Caesar ruled ancient Rome from 49 B.C. until his murder five years later.

CALCULUS see MATH & NUMBERS

CALENDAR

In early history people measured the passing of time by the seasons and changes in the position of the sun and moon. The calendar you use probably works on the same basis. It is divided into years, which represent the time it takes for the earth to orbit, or circle, the sun, and months, which represent the time it takes for the moon to orbit the earth.

The time in Egypt
Over 10,000 years ago the ancient Egyptians had a calendar similar to the modern, Western one. It had 12 months, and each month had 30 days, making a year of 360 days.

However, the earth takes nearly 365¼ days to orbit the sun, so the calendar lost a few days every year. Around 4000 B.C. five extra days were added to each year. This calendar was more accurate but still lost a day every four years.

Other civilizations, such as the Babylonian and the Chinese, also used a system of years containing between 360 and 365 days divided into 12 months. The Jews probably got the idea of a seven-day

A French calendar from about 1450 showing the month of November.

39

dropped leap years in century years unless those years could be divided by 400. Thus 2000 was a leap year, but 1900 was not. The start of the new year was moved from March 25 to January 1. This was known as the Gregorian, or New Style, calendar. It took many years for non-Catholic countries to adopt this calendar. North America and Britain took it up in 1752, but Greece switched only in 1923.

As a result of this historians must take care when looking at dates in the biographies of people who lived through the change. For example, George Washington was born on February 11, 1731 (old style), but on February 22, 1732, under the New Style calendar.

From the 500s onward the Christian church numbered years from the date of

The earliest calendars were circular in shape. This is a reconstruction of a calendar from the Central American Aztec civilization.

week from the Babylonians. The Roman calendar—which forms the basis of most modern systems of time measurement—was in turn based on the Jewish system.

Julian and Gregorian calendars
From the second century B.C. the Romans gave their calendar a 12-month system. However, their year had only 355 days, and this put the calendar out of sequence with the sun. In 46 B.C. Julius Caesar introduced a 365-day system, with an extra day every four years (leap year). It became known as the Julian calendar.

But the Julian calendar was still not a perfect match with the seasons. So in A.D. 1582 Pope Gregory XIII adopted a new calendar that led to the "disappearance" of 10 days in order to bring the year back into line with the seasons. The pope also

DID YOU KNOW?

Most of the names in English for the days of the week come from the ancient Germanic and Norse tribes of northern Europe.

Sunday	Sunnadag, *"Day of the sun."*
Monday	Monandag, *"Day of the moon."*
Tuesday	Tiu, the god of war.
Wednesday	Odin, or Wotan, ruler of the gods.
Thursday	Thor, god of thunder.
Friday	Frigga, wife of Odin.
Saturday	Saturn, Roman god of agriculture.

the birth of Jesus Christ. Years after this date are labeled A.D. (*Anno Domini*, the Latin for "in the year of our Lord"). Those before it are called B.C. (before Christ).

Other calendars today

Today the Gregorian is the most widely used calendar, but there are others. The Chinese calendar puts its years in groups of 12, each named after an animal—rat, ox, tiger, sheep, rabbit, dragon, snake, horse, monkey, rooster, dog, and pig.

The Hebrew calendar of the Jewish religion begins 3,760 years before A.D. 1, and the Islamic calendar begins 622 years after it, with the flight of Muhammad from Mecca to Medina.

SEE ALSO: Ancient Civilizations; Aztecs; Caesar, Julius; Egypt, Ancient; Holiday & Festival; Islam; Judaism; Time

CALIFORNIA

The third largest state is the wealthiest and most populous. It is bordered by Oregon, Nevada, and Arizona, the Pacific Ocean, and Mexico.

California's climate and geography are very varied, from the rainy mountains in the north to the Mojave and Colorado deserts, the biggest in the United States, in the southeast.

Other natural features include Death Valley, the lowest point in the country, and the Sierra Nevada, a range of snowy mountains. Two great geological fault lines—the San Andreas and Hayward faults—run through the state, making it constantly at risk of earthquakes. There are also a higher than average number of floods, mudslides, and forest fires.

The summers are almost without rain. In the winter northern California receives more rain than the south, which averages about 17 in. (432mm) a year. Winter temperatures are mild; in summer the coastline is usually cool, but the desert areas of the southeast are extremely hot for much of the year.

Plant and animal life

Forty percent of California is covered by forests, notably of redwoods and giant sequoia. The state is second only to Oregon in the production of softwoods. Cacti and yucca bloom in the desert. At least 400 species of mammals and

reptiles and 600 types of birds make their homes in California. The California condor, North America's largest land bird, has almost vanished.

History

California takes its name from a book written in the 16th century. It told of Queen Calafía and her mythical kingdom, California. In 1542 Juan Rodríguez Cabrillo explored the California coast. At this time Native American tribes had lived in the area for more than 12,000 years. Cabrillo claimed the land for Spain and named it California. It came

A prospector pans for gold in a river in California. The search for this precious metal sparked massive development in the state during the mid-1800s.

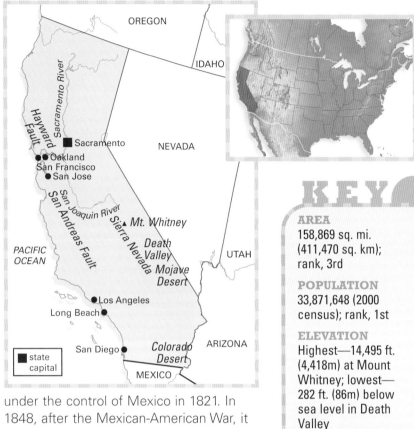

California's state flag

KEY FACTS

AREA
158,869 sq. mi.
(411,470 sq. km);
rank, 3rd

POPULATION
33,871,648 (2000
census); rank, 1st

ELEVATION
Highest—14,495 ft.
(4,418m) at Mount
Whitney; lowest—
282 ft. (86m) below
sea level in Death
Valley

CAPITAL
Sacramento

STATEHOOD
September 9, 1850;
31st state

ABBREVIATION
CA

STATE MOTTO
Eureka (I have
found it)

STATE SONG
"I Love You,
California"

**STATE
NICKNAME**
Golden State

STATE FLOWER
Golden poppy

STATE TREE
California redwood

STATE BIRD
California valley
quail

under the control of Mexico in 1821. In 1848, after the Mexican-American War, it became part of the United States.

In 1849 gold was discovered in California, and many prospectors went there in the hope of making their fortunes. They were nicknamed "forty-niners" after the year they began their adventure. After the Civil War (1861–65) dams and irrigation projects helped improve agriculture. The transcontinental railroad was completed in 1869, opening links with the rest of the country.

During the Great Depression of the 1930s California was the destination for many poor farmers from the Midwest who had been driven off their land by drought. In the following years millions of people came to live in California from the rest of the United States and abroad. One-third of California's residents are Hispanic, with 10 percent Asian American and 7 percent African American.

California today

California has the most urban population in the United States, with 93 percent of its people living in or near cities. The largest cities are Los Angeles (with 16.4 million people, the biggest city in the western United States), San Diego, San Jose, and San Francisco.

An evening panorama of Los Angeles, the largest city in California.

California is home to 10 percent of the nation's workforce. It is the most important state for manufacturing and contains rich mineral resources. The state is also the country's leading agricultural producer—the most fertile areas are the Sacramento and San Joaquin valleys. The main crops are grapes, oranges, tomatoes, and lettuce.

Hollywood is the capital of the film industry, and Silicon Valley, near San Jose, is a world center for computing technology. If California were an independent nation, it would be among the 10 biggest economies in the world.

Desert vegetation in the arid landscape of Death Valley, California.

SEE ALSO: Civil War; Depression, Great; Earthquake; Movies

CAMBODIA see ASIA, SOUTHEAST

CAMEL see MAMMAL, HOOFED

CAMEROON see AFRICA, WEST

CAMOUFLAGE

Some camouflage is simply a matter of color. Polar bears have white coats that make them difficult to spot in the snow and ice of their Arctic habitat. Other species have coats that change with the seasons. Some varieties of weasel have brown coats in summer, then grow white coats when the winter snows come.

Some fish, such as tuna and herring, are darker on the tops of their bodies than on their undersides. When they are viewed from above, their dark backs blend in with the dark water below. When they are viewed from below, the light color of their undersides blends with the brighter water nearer the surface.

Patterned coats can also act as camouflage. The stripes of zebras break up the outline of their bodies and make them difficult for predators to spot. The patterned coats of big cats such as tigers and jaguars make them difficult to see in dappled sunlight and allow them to stalk their prey more easily.

Protective camouflage
Some creatures take on a shape that resembles natural features around them. Many caterpillars and walking stick insects resemble leaves or twigs, and that enables them to hide from predators.

This stick insect is camouflaged to blend in with the branch it is walking along.

Other animals protect themselves by imitating more dangerous species. The hornet fly, for example, has no sting; but because it resembles a hornet, which does sting, birds avoid it.

Camouflage helps animals survive. If they are killed by predators or starve because they cannot catch prey, they will not breed and will not pass on their genes, or unique characteristics. If they live long enough to give birth, they will pass on to their offspring the genes that carry information about camouflage.

▲

The cheetah's spotted fur enables it to blend into its surroundings, giving it an advantage when stalking prey.

SEE ALSO: Evolution; Genetics; Habitat

✳ CANADA

Canada, in northern North America, is the second largest country in the world, after Russia. Most of its land is very sparsely populated.

Canada has coastlines on three oceans, the Atlantic, the Pacific, and the Arctic. Its border with the United States crosses four of the five Great Lakes and Niagara Falls. Canada contains one-third of all the frozen fresh water on Earth.

The landscape includes the Interior Plains, or prairies, part of the North American Great Plains, and the northern part of the Rocky Mountains. Other areas include the Pacific Ranges and Lowlands, and the Arctic Islands, which cover more than 500,000 sq. mi. (1.3 million sq. km).

Canada tends to have cold winters and moderately warm summers. In the far north temperatures fall below 0°F (–18°C) for five months of the year. Snowfall can reach 118 in. (300cm) a year. On the east and west coasts there is more rain—as much as 265 in. (6,700cm) on Vancouver Island, British Columbia.

Plant and animal life

Canada's most important plants are trees. There are about 150 native species, including maple, Douglas fir, Sitka spruce, ponderosa pine, and aspen. One-quarter of Canada is covered by Arctic tundra, where no trees grow. The most common plants here are lichen and moss. About 15 percent of the country is covered by wetland—bogs, swamps, and marshes.

The earliest industry in Canada was the animal fur and skin trade. Hunted animals included beavers, lynxes, mink, polar bears, seals, and walruses. Bison were hunted so much that they are now protected and live on reserves in Alberta and the Northwest Territories.

(Continued on page 46)

Sea lions resting on a rock in the Pacific Ocean off the coast of British Columbia, Canada.
▶

Canada's national flag

ARCTIC OCEAN

Ellesmere Island

Queen Elizabeth Islands

Beaufort Sea

Baffin Bay

GREENLAND (DENMARK)

ALASKA (U.S)

Banks Island

Arctic Islands

Victoria Island

Baffin Island

YUKON TERRITORY

Mackenzie River

Great Bear Lake

Mt. Logan

Whitehorse

NORTHWEST TERRITORIES

Davis Strait

Gulf of Alaska

Pacific Ranges

Yellowknife

NUNAVUT

Hudson Strait

Labrador Sea

BRITISH COLUMBIA

Rocky Mountains

Great Slave Lake

Iqaluit

Lake Athabasca

Hudson Bay

Coast Mountains

ALBERTA

NEWFOUNDLAND

Fraser River

SASKATCHEWAN

MANITOBA

Lowlands

St. John's

Edmonton

Lake Winnipeg

James Bay

QUEBEC

Gulf of St. Lawrence

PACIFIC OCEAN

Vancouver

Interior Plains

ONTARIO

Charlottetown

Victoria

Regina

Fredericton

Prince Edward Island

Winnipeg

Québec City

NOVA SCOTIA

Lake Superior

Ottawa

Halifax

UNITED STATES

Lake Huron

Toronto

Lake Ontario

NEW BRUNSWICK

Lake Michigan

Lake Erie

Niagara Falls

ATLANTIC OCEAN

The largest and most populous city in Canada, Toronto is the country's financial and commercial center. It stands on the shore of Lake Ontario.

Other native animals include grizzly and black bears, cougars, and coyotes. Caribou and reindeer graze on the northern tundra. Fish include walleye, salmon, lake trout, pike, bass, and sturgeon; birds include mallard, American black duck, osprey, bald eagle, red-winged blackbird, and the Canada goose.

People

The largest group of Canadians is of British ancestry (about 28 percent of the population). The next largest group is French-speaking people (about 23 percent). Recently, large numbers of

Europeans trading with native Canadians during the 1700s.

immigrants have come from Asia, especially Hong Kong, India, China, Taiwan, and the Philippines, and from the Caribbean. Today native peoples make up only about 4 percent of the population.

Much of Canada's vast land area is unsuitable for human habitation, and 85 percent of the population lives within 180 miles (300km) of the U.S. border. More than one-quarter of the population lives in Toronto, Montreal, or Vancouver, the three biggest cities.

Economy

Service industries, including tourism, make up the largest segment of Canada's economy. Other major industries include manufacturing, especially in Ontario and Quebec provinces. Agriculture and fishing are concentrated in the Great Lakes–St.

Lawrence Lowlands and the Prairie Provinces. There are rich mineral resources throughout the country.

History

The earliest inhabitants of Canada were Inuits, who arrived from Asia about 25,000 years ago. Leif Eriksson, a Viking explorer, probably landed in northern Newfoundland in about 1000 B.C., but it was another 500 years before there was any permanent European settlement.

In 1497 the Italian Giovanni Caboto (John Cabot) reached Newfoundland. Many fishermen followed, attracted by the massive stocks of fish in the northwestern Atlantic Ocean. In 1534 Jacques Cartier claimed the Gulf of St. Lawrence for France and named the area Kanata, from the Huron-Iroquois word for "village" or "settlement."

By the end of the 1500s French and English settlers were competing for the fur trade. Humphrey Gilbert claimed Newfoundland for England in 1583, and Samuel de Champlain founded Quebec, a French settlement, in 1608. By 1689 the French, assisted by the Hurons, were in open conflict with the English and their Iroquois allies. Peace returned in 1713 when France surrendered Acadia (now Nova Scotia), Newfoundland, and Hudson Bay. The 1750s brought further disagreements that ended only when the French forces surrendered at Montreal in 1760. Canada was now British.

French people in a British state

There was still a large minority of French-speaking settlers in Canada, and the Quebec Act of 1774 gave them legal and religious rights. American colonists were angry that land they planned to settle was now subject to French law. The act became one of the causes of the American Revolution. Americans tried to invade Canada in 1775 and again in 1812.

The Act of Union in 1840 united the two territories of Upper and Lower Canada (now Ontario and Quebec). In 1867 the British North America Act created the Canadian Confederation, comprising Ontario, Quebec, New Brunswick, and Nova Scotia. The first prime minister of Canada was John A. Macdonald.

In the 1880s a métis (part-French, part-Native American) called Louis Riel led the Northwest Rebellion of prairie settlers unhappy at the pace of westward confederation. Riel was executed in 1885, but he became a figurehead for French-speakers who were unhappy at the increasing power of the Canadian state.

In 1905 the new provinces of Alberta and Saskatchewan were created.

Postwar Canada

After World War II (1939–45) Canadian French-speakers campaigned to make Quebec independent from Canada. The separatist Parti Québécois took control of the province in 1976, but gave up calls for full independence in 1995.

In 1982 the Constitution Act finally granted Canada the right to amend its own constitution without permission from Britain.

The western red cedar is one of many magnificent species of tree native to Canada.

Niagara Falls forms part of the border between the United States and Canada.

An aerial view of Long Beach in the Pacific Rim National Park, British Columbia, Canada.

In 1994 Canada signed the North American Free Trade Agreement (NAFTA) with the United States and Mexico.

In 1999 Nunavut was created as Canada's newest territory, a homeland for the Inuit people. Located in the high Arctic part of the Northwest Territories, the capital of Nunavut is Iqaluit.

SEE ALSO: Alberta; British Columbia; Exploration & Explorers; French & Indian War; Inuit; Manitoba; New Brunswick; Newfoundland; Northwest Territories; Nova Scotia; Nunavut; Ontario; Prince Edward Island; Quebec; Revolution, American; Saskatchewan; Viking; Yukon Territory

✳ CANAL

Canals are artificial channels or ditches filled with water. They were built originally to drain swamps or irrigate dry land.

A container ship passes through the 100-mile (160km) Suez Canal in Egypt.

Early in history people found another important use for canals—transportation. A canal can join two cities. It can give inland areas access to the sea. Rivers, lakes, and seas can be linked by canals to provide shorter or safer water routes.

Canals can be built all on one level, or they can go from one level to another by means of locks. Locks are sections of a canal with watertight gates at each end. A ship going from a lower to a higher level in a canal sails into a lock through its open lower gates. The gates are shut behind it. Water is then allowed to flow into the lock until the level of water inside it is as high as the water in the upper level of the canal. Finally the upper gates are opened, and the ship goes on its way. If a ship is going down to a lower level, the process is simply turned around, and water is let out through small openings in the gates. If the gates themselves were opened to let water in or out, a torrent would rush in or out with terrific force, damaging the ship or washing away the canal banks. If ships need to go up or down a great height, more than one lock is used.

History of canals

Nearly 4,000 years ago the ancient Egyptians built one of the earliest known canals for transportation. It connected the Nile River with the Red Sea. Ships could travel from the Mediterranean to the Red Sea by sailing along the Nile and through the canal. The world's greatest canal system is the Grand Canal of China, which was completed in around A.D. 620. Including its side branches, it stretches more than 1,678 miles (2,700km).

One of the most famous artificial waterways of modern times is the Suez Canal, built in Egypt between 1859 and 1869 to link the Mediterranean and the Red seas. It enabled ships to go from Europe to Asia without having to sail around Africa.

The Panama Canal, completed in 1914, links the Atlantic and Pacific oceans, eliminating the long trip around the southern tip of South America.

SEE ALSO:
China;
Egypt,
Ancient;
Panama

✳ CAPE VERDE 👉 ✳ AFRICA, WEST

✳ CAPITALISM 👉 ✳ ECONOMY

✳ CAR

The first self-powered road vehicle was built by a Frenchman, Nicolas Cugnot, in 1769. It was a three-wheeled steam engine designed to pull cannons. It was never fully tested because it crashed during a trial run.

Later efforts by the Englishman Richard Trevithick and the American Oliver Evans had little success. It was not until the late 1800s that the car as we now know it began to take shape.

The German engineers Gottlieb Daimler and Karl Benz both created working, engine-driven automobiles in 1886. In the 1890s French engineer Emile Levassor built a car with spring suspension and clutch-and-gear transmission. The next big idea was the brainchild of the Americans Ransom E. Olds and Henry M. Leland, who found it profitable to build all their vehicles from standardized parts.

The greatest advances in car manufacture, however, were made by Henry Ford, who developed the assembly line that made mass production possible. In the Ford plant cars under construction were moved down the line on a conveyor belt, and each worker had a few simple tasks to perform, over and over, many times a day.

Henry Ford and his son, Edsel, in the 1905 Model F Ford outside their home in Detroit, Michigan.

Cars for the masses

Before the assembly line it took 728 minutes to build a complete chassis. Afterward it took 93 minutes. Between 1908 and 1925 the cost of a Model T fell from $850 to $290. Cars were now affordable by ordinary people.

INSIDE A CAR

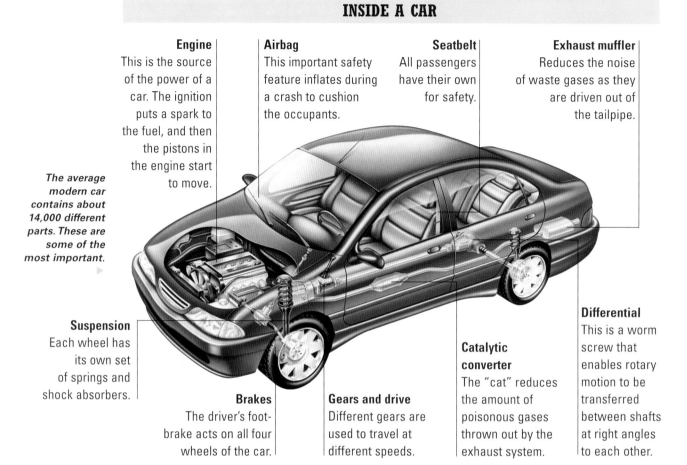

Engine
This is the source of the power of a car. The ignition puts a spark to the fuel, and then the pistons in the engine start to move.

Airbag
This important safety feature inflates during a crash to cushion the occupants.

Seatbelt
All passengers have their own for safety.

Exhaust muffler
Reduces the noise of waste gases as they are driven out of the tailpipe.

The average modern car contains about 14,000 different parts. These are some of the most important.
▶

Suspension
Each wheel has its own set of springs and shock absorbers.

Brakes
The driver's foot-brake acts on all four wheels of the car.

Gears and drive
Different gears are used to travel at different speeds.

Catalytic converter
The "cat" reduces the amount of poisonous gases thrown out by the exhaust system.

Differential
This is a worm screw that enables rotary motion to be transferred between shafts at right angles to each other.

In the next few decades developments such as hydraulic brakes, safety glass, and car radios made driving safer and more enjoyable. Large numbers of trucks were built to carry goods.

By the 1960s the massive increase in car use was causing pollution problems. Laws were passed to control the chemicals that cars pumped into the air. In the 1970s there were gasoline shortages, and manufacturers made cars smaller and more efficient. More recently, battery-powered cars have been developed to protect the Earth's resources, but they are still not generally used.

Although cars provide many benefits to society, they have several disadvantages, including congestion and pollution.

How a car works
Most cars are powered by internal combustion engines. They are started up by an electrical system that makes a spark and powered by liquid fuel—either gasoline or diesel. When mixed with air and burned, the fuel generates expanding gases. The gases are a form of energy

AMAZING FACTS!

In the United States there are about two people per car; in China there are more than 1,300 people per car.
In a year American motorists travel about 2 trillion miles.
The longest car ever built is a 26-wheel limousine, 100 ft. (30.5m) long.

that is used to turn a shaft. The torque, or twisting force, of this shaft is used to turn the car's driving wheels.

The transmission, or gearbox, of a car uses coupling devices and sets of gears to match the engine's rotating speed to the desired road speed. The device that controls the transmission is called the clutch. Transmissions may be automatic or manual, with the shifting of gears and pressing of the clutch pedal being carried out by the driver.

Oil protects the various engine parts from rubbing against each other, and a cooling system prevents overheating. The exhaust removes waste gases.

The suspension is a set of springs and shock absorbers that soften unevenness in the road and help the car take corners smoothly and safely.

Today most cars are built with safety features, such as airbags. Yet thousands of people are still killed and injured on the road each year. The car provides many benefits, but it must be used with care.

SEE ALSO: Engine; Pollution; Transportation

✳ CARIBBEAN SEA AND ISLANDS

Named for the Carib Indians, who once inhabited some of the islands, the Caribbean Sea covers an area of about 750,000 sq. mi. (about 2 million sq. km). The Panama Canal links the Caribbean with the Pacific Ocean, making the sea one of the world's major waterways.

Island groups
The islands of the Caribbean consist of two main groups: the Greater Antilles and the Lesser Antilles. The Greater Antilles include the four largest islands—Cuba, Hispaniola (shared by the nations of Haiti and the Dominican Republic), Jamaica, and Puerto Rico. The Lesser Antilles include Barbados, the Leeward Islands, and the Windward Islands. The Virgin Islands and the northern islands of the Netherlands Antilles are usually classified as parts of the Lesser Antilles. To the north the Bahamas and the Turks and Caicos Islands are outside the Caribbean area.

Land and climate
The islands are part of two partly submerged mountain chains that reach their highest point in Hispaniola. The mountains have been worn away on many of the Lesser Antilles, but some of the other islands still have active volcanoes.

The Caribbean region has a moderate climate, cooled by the breezes of the trade

Downtown Kingston, the capital of Jamaica and the home of reggae music.

FLORIDA (U.S.)

Gulf of Mexico

BAHAMAS

ATLANTIC OCEAN

TURKS & CAICOS ISLANDS (BR.)

CUBA

CAYMAN ISLANDS

HAITI

JAMAICA

DOMINICAN REPUBLIC

PUERTO RICO (U.S.)

VIRGIN ISLANDS (U.S./BR.)

LEEWARD ISLANDS

BARBADOS

HONDURAS

Caribbean Sea

NICARAGUA

NETHERLANDS ANTILLES

WINDWARD ISLANDS

TRINIDAD & TOBAGO

COSTA RICA

COLOMBIA

VENEZUELA

winds. Temperatures range from about 70 to 85°F (21–29°C). Rainfall is heaviest in summer. Hurricanes often develop in the late summer or early fall and may cause widespread damage.

People

St. John, one of the three main U.S. Virgin Islands, which lie about 40 miles (64km) east of Puerto Rico.

The original Indian inhabitants of the islands died out soon after the arrival of European settlers. Most Caribbean peoples today are descended from Africans brought to the region to work as slaves on fruit and sugar plantations. The varied languages of the islands include English, Spanish, French, and Dutch.

KEY FACTS

GREATER ANTILLES
Cuba, Hispaniola (Haiti and the Dominican Republic), Jamaica, Puerto Rico (U.S.)

LESSER ANTILLES
Anguilla (Br.), Antigua and Barbuda, Aruba (Neth.), Barbados, Bonaire (Neth.), Curaçao (Neth.), Dominica, Grenada, Guadeloupe (Fr.), Martinique (Fr.), Montserrat (Br.), Saba (Neth.), St. Eustatius (Neth.), St. Kitts and Nevis, St. Lucia, St. Martin (Fr.-Neth.), St.

Vincent and the Grenadines, Trinidad and Tobago, British Virgin Islands, U.S. Virgin Islands (St. Croix, St. John, St. Thomas)

OTHER ISLANDS
Cayman Islands (Br.), Margarita (Venez.), Tortuga (Venez.)

STATUS
All Caribbean islands are independent except where noted:
Br. = Britain
Fr. = France
Neth. = Netherlands
U.S. = United States
Venez. = Venezuela

Economy

For centuries the chief products of the Caribbean have been sugar, coffee, tropical fruits, and spices. However, industry is now Puerto Rico's main source of income. Curaçao and Trinidad have petroleum refineries. Cuba has one of the world's largest deposits of nickel, and Jamaica produces bauxite, the chief source of aluminum. Tourism is an important industry for all the islands.

History

Christopher Columbus reached the Caribbean in 1492. The Spanish then colonized the Greater Antilles. For the next 300 years Spain vied with other European nations for dominance in the region. The Caribbean was also a profitable hunting ground for pirates.

As a result of the Spanish-American War (1898), Cuba won its independence, and Puerto Rico became a territory of the United States. In 1917 the United States bought St. Croix, St. John, and St. Thomas (the U.S. Virgin Islands) from Denmark.

Haiti was the first Caribbean state to gain independence, following a revolt against the French in the late 1700s. The Dominican Republic gained independence from Spain in the mid-1800s, and Cuba became a republic in 1902. Most of the British-owned islands became independent between 1960 and 1980.

SEE ALSO:
Columbus, Christopher;
Cuba;
Music, Popular;
Panama

✳ CARNIVORE

Scientists divide animals into groups called orders. The order Carnivora is made up of the mammals that eat meat.

Ten families make up the Carnivora: dogs, wolves, foxes, and jackals; bears; racoons and pandas; weasels, skunks, otters, and badgers; genets, civets, and mongooses; hyenas; cats; sea lions; seals; and walrus.

Hunting

Meat-eating animals spend much of their time seeking the food they need to survive. A few meat-eating animals do not hunt for themselves; instead, they clean up the remains of animals killed by other creatures. Such animals are called scavengers and include hyenas.

The hunting styles of carnivores are related to the type of prey on which they feed. Wolves and cheetahs hunt fast-running, four-legged herbivores (plant eaters). In a matter of three seconds the cheetah can reach speeds of almost 70 mph (113km/h), but only for a brief time. If

After they have killed their prey, gray wolves fight among themselves as they struggle for dominance within the pack. The strongest eat first.
▶

the cheetah does not catch its prey within about 600 ft. (185m), it gives up and looks for another victim. Wolves hunt in packs. Members take turns chasing their victims and can keep up pursuit for miles. The prey becomes exhausted and an easy target for the hungry pack.

Meat eaters have long, sharp teeth for tearing and chewing flesh, and strong jaws. The curved, sharp claws of cats are used to grab and hold prey. They can withdraw, or retract, their claws when they are not needed for this purpose. That enables them to step softly when stalking prey. Cats—from house cats to lions—like to creep up close to their intended victims before they pounce.

Bears are the largest land carnivores. They live mainly on insects, seeds, nuts, plants, and berries; some also eat fish. Only the polar bear lives mainly on meat, principally seals. Pandas are carnivores, but they live mostly on bamboo shoots, while racoons are carnivores that eat almost anything. The sea otter eats

Sea otters are carnivorous mammals that feed mainly on shellfish.

AMAZING FACTS !

The elephant seal, the largest carnivore, can weigh 4 tons (3,600kg). **The least weasel**, the smallest carnivore, weighs only 1–2½ oz. (30–70g).

abalone and other shellfish, which it opens by cracking them on a rock held on its chest as it floats in the water.

Reproduction
Most carnivores have between three and six young. Bears usually have two cubs. The Asiatic polecat may have up to 18 young. Most young are cared for by one or both parents until they have learned to hunt and so can fend for themselves.

SEE ALSO:
Bear; Cat; Dog; Herbivore; Sea Mammal

Look in the Index for: ✳CARROLL, LEWIS

✵ SET INDEX

Numbers in **bold type** are volume numbers. Page numbers in *italics* refer to pictures or their captions.

PICTURE CREDITS
l = left r = right, t = top c = center b = bottom ba = background

AKG London: 39, VISI OARS 8,19t; **ARS/USDA:** Scott Bauer 12b; **Art Explosion:** 18b; **Bruce Coleman Collection:** Gunter Ziesler 5b; **Chandra X-Ray Center:** A. Hobart 19b; **Corbis:** Tiziana & Gianni Baldizzone 21b, Bettmann 20t, 32, 41, 49, Christie's Images 22, Duomo 4, Ecoscene 16b, Owen Franken 24b, Steve Kaufman 43b, Alain Le Garsmeur 51, Gianni Dagli Orti 23b, 40, Brian A.Vikander 44t; **Daimler Chrysler:** 10t; **Edgar Fah Smith Collection, University of Pennsylvania Library:** 13c; **George Bush Library:** 35; **Getty Images:** 11t, 34, AEF/Yves Debay 48b, Jeff Cadge 10b, Derek Berwin 27, Gary Cralle 45, Steve Dunwell 52, Eddie Hironaka 42, Tony Lewis 3l, Kevin Schafer 54, Pete Seward 50, TimeLife Pictures/MAI/Sandy Schaeffer 20b, Art Wolfe 53; **Hemera**

Technologies Inc.: 3r, 9; **ImageState:** 29, 33, Brian Lawrence 47b, Jeffery Rich 16t; **Mary Evans Picture Library:** 7t,13t, 25, 46; **NHPA:** Christophe Ratier 26; **PA Photos:** AFP/Fabian Gredillas 13b, EPA 7b,12t, 28, 36; **Photodisc:** 15b, 30, Alan & Sandy Carey 18t, Don Farrall 6, Geostock 17t, Robert Glusic 38, PhotoLink 17b, /D.Falconer 15t; **RCA:** 24t; **Rex Features Ltd:** 11b; **Still Pictures:** Mark Edwards 14, Roland Seitre 5t, Gordon Wiltsie 43t; **Tourism British Columbia:** 44b, 47t, 48t; **Werner Forman Archive:** 37, The British Library, London 23t **Cover: Photodisc** ba; **Daimler Chrysler** r; **Tourism British Columbia** l.